Chef Dez on Cooking

Volume 1

Note for Librarians: A cataloguing record for this book is available from Library and Archives Canada at www.collectionscanada.ca/amicus/index-e.html
ISBN 1-4251-2019-9

Printed in Victoria, BC, Canada. Printed on paper with minimum 30% recycled fibre.
Trafford's print shop runs on "green energy" from solar, wind and other environmentally-friendly power sources.

Offices in Canada, USA, Ireland and UK

Book sales for North America and international:
Trafford Publishing, 6E–2333 Government St.,
Victoria, BC V8T 4P4 CANADA
phone 250 383 6864 (toll-free 1 888 232 4444)
fax 250 383 6804; email to orders@trafford.com
Book sales in Europe:
Trafford Publishing (UK) Limited, 9 Park End Street, 2nd Floor
Oxford, UK OX1 1HH UNITED KINGDOM
phone +44 (0)1865 722 113 (local rate 0845 230 9601)
facsimile +44 (0)1865 722 868; info.uk@trafford.com
Order online at:
trafford.com/07-0423

10 9 8 7 6 5 4 3

For Katherine, my soul mate...
and Sous Chef

*T*o reduce the cost of this book to you, the consumer, colour photos for the following recipes available for viewing/printing on my website at:

www.chefdez.com

Amaretto Truffles with Vanilla Pastry Cream
Bacon & Cheddar Corn Chowder
Bacon Wrapped Asparagus
Blueberry Cheesecake Crêpes
Bocconcini Salad with Balsamic Reduction
Cajun Chicken with Black Bean Succotash
Cajun Chicken with Kiwi Salsa
Canapés for All Occasions
Cheddar Apple Turnovers
Cherry Citrus Liqueur
Chicken Provençale
Chili-Rubbed Chicken & Cornbread
Chocolate Covered Strawberries

Cinnamon Roasted Pork Tenderloin with Pinot Gris Applesauce
Coq au Vin
Cranberry Almond Coffee Cake
Cranberry Pistachio Banana Bread
Creamy Lime Custard Pie
Creamy Stuffed Eggplant
Easy BBQ Pig Sandwich
Fat Free Sweet Potato Bisque
Garlic & Red Wine Braised Beef with Ham & Gruyère Cheese
Greek Salad
Greek Souvlaki
Grilled Brie & Apple Pizza
Indian Butter Chicken
Italian Polenta Buns with Grappa
Linguine Puttanesca
Loaded Nachos
Marscapone Stuffed Poached Pears
Mediterranean Stuffed Pork Loin Roast
Mom's Cherry Soup
Mushroom Omelet
Parsley Pesto
Poached Salmon with No Fat Yogurt Dill Sauce
Rack of Lamb with Rosemary Roasted Potatoes
Roasted Garlic & Tomato Bruscetta
Roasted Greek Potatoes
Royal Apples (Apple Dumplings)
Scampi
Southwestern Steak Diane
Spanikopita
Stacked Eggplant Appy
Steamed Mussels in Red Wine & Garlic
Strawberry Passoire à la Crème
Sweet Potato Spinach Patties with Pomegranate Demi-Glaze
Tomato Mushroom Rosé Pasta Sauce
Tomato Rosé Pasta Sauce

Acknowledgments

This project has been a long time in the making, and I apologize to the many that have been patiently anticipating. After a few "speed bumps" along the way *Chef Dez on Cooking, Volume 1* is finally a reality.

This book could never have happened with out the wonderful support and hard work from my wife Katherine. She was always there in the kitchen with me frantically jotting down ingredients/instructions as I was creating. She is a tremendous cook and her input is the most valuable resource I could ask for. As a matter of fact, she heads up the recipes in *"Chapter 12 – Pies for Holiday Desserts"* and I am certain you will enjoy her creations. Katherine, thank you Sweetheart for your help, understanding, and encouragement through this project.

Support from my children Corey, Krista, and Noah played a large part in the creation of this book as well. There were many times that I was either confined to the kitchen or had my nose pressed to the computer screen. Your understanding means a lot to me and has not gone unnoticed.

Huge thanks also to my Mom. She was the main influence during my upbringing and the one responsible for my passion for food since I was a young child. We have eaten many favorite recipes together and I thank you for all of your love and support.

Angie at *Well Seasoned Gourmet Food Store* has been a huge supporter of me and I appreciate everything she has done. She has always booked me into her incredible store to teach, and always welcomes me with a cup of hot coffee and a smile. The time she has taken out of her busy life to write the Foreword of this book speaks volumes of the support she gives to me. Thank you Angie.

There have also been a number of other venues, that I have had the honor of teaching at, that deserve recognition as well: Limbert Mountain Farm, Kapestro's Restaurant, Lotus Land Vineyards, Abbotsford Community School, and Mission Parks and Recreation.

Gratitude to all of the venues I have performed shows at: West Coast Women's Show, Cloverdale Rodeo, Gotta-be-Kiddin Family Expo, Minter Gardens, and especially the Abbotsford Agrifair where I perform 16 shows every year during the August long weekend.

A great appreciation also to the following: Trafford Publishing, Wendy Gilmour of Gilmour Promotions, Anya Wilson Publicity, Julie Van Rosendaal, Rod Thomson, Aaron Pritchett, George Canyon, Beverly Hudson, and all of the Editors and Publishers of *Chef Dez on Cooking* for the ongoing support they have given me.

Lastly, I want to thank everyone who has attended my classes, welcomed me into their homes, attended my cooking shows, and has been a dedicated reader of my columns. Without you… none of this would be a reality. Thank you so much.

Table of Contents

Chef Dez comes to the rescue with amazingly simple skills for culinary success and mouthwatering recipes that anyone can master. From Apples to Zest, Dez's friendly voice says: "Come into the kitchen with me, let's cook. And don't forget the garlic!"

This passionate and engaging culinary king wants us all back at the kitchen table, where friends and family come together, sharing time and breaking bread. He wants everyone to learn to cook fantastic food with ease and pride: to make cooking a truly satisfying experience.

I was thrilled and honoured when Dez asked me to write the forward for his cookbook. He has been a culinary instructor in my business, Well Seasoned ~ a gourmet food store, since we opened in May 2004. He has created everything from the world's very best mashed potatoes to his phenomenal Filet Mignon. Besides being one of my favourite people, Dez is a dedicated instructor and gifted chef, with a flair for fabulous food, fun and easy ways to make food look as good as it tastes.

If you have bought this book or have received it as a gift you are in luck – Dez's recipes are easy to follow, sensible and delicious. His flair for instruction makes it all so doable, even for the most inexperienced cook. When you use one of his recipes you can be sure he has painstakingly prepared it over and over to ensure you will be able to recreate it perfectly in your own kitchen.

This straightforward approach to everyday cooking holds a wide variety of mouth-watering, one-of-a-kind recipes you'll want to share with everyone. Chef Dez will spice up your kitchen and your life, and help create new food traditions, just as he has in mine.

Happy cooking & don't forget the garlic,
Angie Quaale
Well Seasoned ~ a gourmet food store
Langley, BC
www.wellseasoned.ca

1

Garlic: Is it our Friend or our Foe?

Being a Chef, I am certain that you will think my opinion is biased when I tell you that garlic is my friend. However, I have reasons to support my love for this little bulb.

I honestly believe that most people, who say they hate the taste of garlic, must have been exposed to an overpowered Caesar dressing or Greek tzatziki sauce at some point in their lives. Garlic, when cooked, does not have that overly pungent flavour reminiscent of these raw form recipes. Alternatively, it has a sweeter and smoother temperament and adds a depth of flavour to your dish that cannot be mimicked.

Garlic is one of the oldest cultivated plants known to mankind and has been hailed as one of world's most celebrated medicinal vegetables. There are many stories of old, that proclaim of its pure powers to increase endurance and stamina. It also has many therapeutic properties. Medical studies have confirmed that garlic contains natural antibiotic and cleansing qualities and it is used to treat a wide range of health problems.

When buying garlic, you want to make sure that that the bulb or "head" is not discoloured and it is tightly wrapped in its own natural paper-like skin. Do not buy garlic that is falling apart, as this is a sure sign of its age. Additionally, stay away from garlic that has little green sprouts coming from the encased cloves – although these are virtually harmless, they do add an unnecessary bitterness to the garlic's natural flavour. If these green sprouts develop in time from the garlic you have already purchased, simply split the clove with a knife and cut out this growth before adding it to your recipe. These little green sprouts are a sign that you are storing your garlic in an area that is too humid. Garlic is best stored in a cool, dry, well-ventilated space and it will keep for several months. It is not recommended that you store garlic in your refrigerator.

I personally cook with and consume garlic on a daily basis. There are many great ways to add this wonderful vegetable to a variety of dishes; just practice "moderation" if the thought of the taste in your recipe scares you. One final note: the sprig of parsley that has been added to enhance the presentation of your plate was originally derived from the practice of chewing it after a meal to freshen one's breath.

> *Dear Chef Dez:*
> *I like the taste of garlic in different dishes, however whenever I add it to a stir-fry it always adds a bitter flavour. What am I doing wrong?*
>
> > *John D.*
> > *Abbotsford, BC*

> *Dear John:*
> *If this is the only time you experience a bitter flavour from the addition of garlic to a recipe, I suspect that it is getting burned. Garlic burns very easily, especially if added to the extreme temperature of oil in "wok cooking". To avoid this problem in the future, always add a different vegetable first to the hot oil to temper it a little before adding the garlic.*

Chicken Provençale

Full colour photo available at www.chefdez.com

"Soaking the chicken breasts in the salt-water brine helps to keep them moist and flavourful"

¼ (one quarter) cup& 2 tbsp table salt
1.5 lbs boneless, skinless chicken breasts (approx. 4 portions)
Flour for dredging
3 tbsp olive oil

CHEF DEZ

1 medium shallot, minced

6 – 8 garlic cloves, minced

1 anchovy, or 1 tsp anchovy paste

2 tsp dried oregano

1 – 28 oz can of diced tomatoes, drained.

1 cup chardonnay, or other white wine

2 tsp white sugar

2 tbsp tomato paste

10 calamata olives, pitted and minced

Fresh oregano leaves for garnish

1. Dissolve the salt in 6 cups cold water. Submerse the chicken breasts in this salt-water brine for 1 ½ (one and one half) hours in the refrigerator.

2. Take chicken out of the brine and pat dry with paper towels. Discard brine. Dredge chicken in flour to lightly coat.

3. Heat a heavy bottomed pan over medium-high heat. Add 2 tbsp of the olive oil and brown the chicken on both sides, approximately 3 minutes per side. Do not crowd the pan – if the pan is too crowded, the chicken will steam in their juices rather than brown. Once browned, remove chicken from pan and set aside.

4. Cool down the pan a bit by adding half of the tomatoes and turn down the heat to medium.

5. Add the third tbsp of olive oil, shallot, garlic, anchovy, and oregano and sauté for about 2 minutes until shallot and garlic are softened.

6. Add the rest of the tomatoes, wine, and the chicken breasts. Turn heat to high and bring to a boil.

7. Reduce the heat to simmer, cover and cook over med-low heat for 20 minutes.

8. Remove the chicken and set aside covered with foil to keep warm.

9. Increase heat to high, add the tomato paste and the sugar. Reduce the liquid by boiling for approximately 5 minutes until it has reached desired consistency, stirring occasionally.

10. Remove the sauce from the heat and stir in the olives. Serve immediately; plate one chicken breast per plate, and spoon sauce over it, and garnish with fresh oregano leaves. Great on its own or serve on rice or pasta

Makes 4 portions

Garlic Mashed Potatoes

"These will spoil you for any other mashed potatoes – very rich and flavourful"

5 russet potatoes, peeled and diced approximated ½ inch
½ (one half) cup butter, cubed
6 – 8 garlic cloves, crushed
2 tsp salt
½ (one half) tsp pepper
½ (one half) cup 35% M.F. whipping cream

1 Steam potatoes over boiling water for approximately 20 minutes until tender.
2 Drain water out of the pot, and put cooked potatoes in the pot.
3 Add the butter, garlic, salt, and pepper.
4 Mash by hand until almost smooth.
5 Add the cream and mash again until smooth.
6 Taste and re-season with salt & pepper if necessary.

Makes approximately 6 – 8 portions

Greek Tzatziki

"A Greek mealtime favorite – serve it on grilled Greek souvlaki or simply use it as a dip for pita bread. Do not peel the cucumbers, as the skin adds a lot of colour!"

1 long English cucumber, grated
500g plain yogurt
3 - 4 garlic cloves, crushed
1 tbsp finely chopped fresh dill
1 tbsp olive oil
salt and pepper to season

1 Put grated cucumbers in a clean towel or cheesecloth and squeeze to remove moisture.
2 Place drained cucumbers in a bowl, and add all the other ingredients; stir to combine.

3 Cover with plastic wrap and refrigerate for a minimum of two hours for the flavours to marry.

Makes approximately 3 cups

Garlic Tarragon Cream Sauce

"Don't be intimidated by the amount of garlic in this recipe. As the garlic cloves cook while the wine and broth reduces, they become very sweet and caramelized."

2 heads of garlic, cloves peeled & left whole
1 cup white wine
1 cup chicken broth
2 cups 35% M.F. whipping cream
1 tsp salt
2 tsp fresh chopped tarragon

1 Put garlic cloves and wine in a heavy bottomed pot, and bring to a boil over medium heat.
2 Turn the heat down to medium/low and simmer until all the liquid has evaporated, stirring occasionally. **Be careful not to burn the garlic.**
3 Once all of the wine has evaporated, add the chicken broth and bring to a boil over medium heat.
4 Turn the heat down to medium/low and simmer until all the broth has evaporated, stirring occasionally. **Be careful not to burn the garlic.**
5 Add the cream and bring to a simmer. Turn down the heat to low and cook for 5 minutes, stirring occasionally.
6 Puree the mixture in a blender or food processor for 30 seconds until garlic cloves have blended into the cream.
7 Return the sauce to the pot. Add the salt and tarragon and warm over low heat for a few minutes, to infuse the tarragon flavour into the sauce.
8 Serve immediately with your favorite pasta or use as a complimenting sauce to any seafood or chicken dish.

Makes approximately 2 cups

Roasted Garlic

"If you don't have an ovenproof casserole dish, simply seal the garlic heads in aluminum foil"

4 heads of garlic
4 tsp olive oil
Salt & pepper

1. Preheat oven to 450 degrees.
2. Keeping the garlic heads whole, cut off the tops of the garlic heads, just enough to cut off the tops of the garlic cloves.
3. Place the heads of garlic in an ovenproof casserole dish equipped with a lid.
4. Drizzle 1 tsp of olive oil over each of the exposed garlic heads. Season lightly with salt and fresh cracked pepper.
5. Cover and bake for 45 minutes.
6. Remove from the oven and let stand at room temperature (with the lid on) until cool enough to touch.
7. Serve whole for presentation, or squeeze out the cloves and mix into a variety of spreads, dips, or sauces.

Roasted Garlic Mayonnaise

"Fantastic on Sandwiches"

1 head roasted garlic
¼ (one quarter) cup mayonnaise
½ (one half) tsp liquid honey

1. Squeeze the cloves of the roasted garlic head into a small bowl. Discard the papery skin.
2. Mash with a fork. Add the mayonnaise and honey. Stir to combine completely.
3. Refrigerate up to 3 days until needed. Great on sandwiches!

Makes approximately 1/3 cup

Roasted Garlic Mediterranean Spread

"Serve on small slices of baguette for a quick & delicious appetizer"

3 – 4 heads roasted garlic
1/3 (one third) cup oil packed sun-dried tomatoes, oil drained & reserved
2 tbsp whole pine nuts
2 tsp balsamic vinegar
1 tsp of the oil drained from the sun-dried tomatoes
½ (one half) tsp liquid honey
Salt & fresh cracked pepper

1 Squeeze the cloves of the roasted garlic heads into a small bowl. Discard the papery skin. Mash with a fork.
2 Finely chop the sun-dried tomatoes and add to the garlic along with the pine nuts, vinegar, oil, and honey. Mix together.

Season to taste with salt and fresh cracked pepper.

Makes approximately 2/3 cup

Roasted Garlic & Tomato Bruscetta

Full colour photo available at www.chefdez.com

"If you can spare the time, the roasting of the tomatoes in this recipe is well worth it – they become so intense in flavour! Make extra tomatoes and add them to pasta, sandwiches, salads, etc."

9 roma tomatoes
2 tbsp olive oil
2 tbsp balsamic vinegar
2 tsp dried basil
2 tsp dried oregano
½ (one half) tsp salt
½ (one half) tsp fresh cracked pepper
5 heads roasted garlic
1 teaspoon liquid honey

1 baguette
150g provolone cheese, sliced thin or grated
18 large cooked prawns

1 Preheat oven to 200 degrees.
2 Remove and discard the green tops of the tomatoes, slice in half from top to bottom (lengthwise), and place them in a mixing bowl.
3 Add the olive oil, balsamic vinegar, basil, oregano, salt, pepper, and toss to coat. Gently work a small amount of pulp out of tomato halves while working the flavourings into the tomato cavities.
4 Arrange the tomatoes cut side up on a baking sheet lined with parchment paper.
5 Spoon the remaining liquid from the bowl over the tomatoes and lightly season each one again with salt and pepper.
6 Bake for approximately 5 to 6 hours, until the tomatoes have reduced by approximately two-thirds in size but are still moist. Cool to room temperature and cut each tomato half into two pieces.
7 Squeeze the cloves of garlic from the heads into a small mixing bowl. Stir in the honey and season to taste with salt and pepper.
8 Slice the baguette diagonally into 18 slices. Lay them on a baking sheet and toast in a 450 degree oven until brown; flip them over and toast opposite side and remove from oven.
9 Turn the oven to broil. Leaving the baguette slices on the baking sheet divide the roasted garlic spread evenly on the baguette slices.
10 Top each bruscetta with a two tomato pieces (one half tomato) and provolone cheese.
11 Broil in the oven until cheese has melted.
12 Top each one with a large prawn and serve immediately.

Makes 18 bruscetta

CHEF DEZ

Roasted Greek Potatoes

Full colour photo available at www.chefdez.com

"It is important to use a metal baking pan – it attracts more heat than glass casserole dishes. The darker the pan, the more heat it will attract to brown the potatoes properly!"

5 large Russet potatoes, peeled
½ (one half) cup fresh lemon juice
1 whole head of garlic, chopped
1 tbsp dried oregano
¼ (one quarter) cup olive oil
Salt & fresh cracked pepper to season
Chopped lemon zest and fresh parsley for garnish, optional

1. Preheat the oven to 400 degrees.
2. Cut the potatoes into thirds or quarters, depending on how large they are.
3. Place all ingredients in a metal baking pan and mix to coat.
4. Bake until tender, approximately 1 hour, turning and coating every 15 minutes.
5. Lightly re-season with salt immediately after they are removed from the oven. Let cool 5 to 10 minutes before serving.

Serves 6 to 8 as a side dish

Steamed Mussels in Red Wine & Garlic

Full colour photo available at www.chefdez.com

"Very easy to make! Serve with big chunks of crusty bread to soak up the broth."

30 – 36 live mussels
1 tbsp olive oil
28 fl oz. can of diced tomatoes, drained
1 head of garlic, peeled and minced
2 tsp white sugar
Salt & fresh cracked pepper

1 cup red wine

¼ (one quarter) cup fresh chopped parsley (plus more for garnish)

Lemon slices or wedges

1 Clean and de-beard the mussels.
2 Heat heavy bottomed large pan over medium-high heat. Add the olive oil, tomatoes, and garlic, and season with the sugar, salt & fresh cracked pepper. Sauté for about 1 – 2 minutes.
3 Add the red wine and bring to a boil.
4 Add the mussels and parsley; cover with a lid and steam until the mussels open.
5 Remove from the heat. Taste and re-season with salt and pepper, if necessary.
6 Garnish with lemon and extra fresh parsley.

Makes 4 portions as an appetizer, or 2 portions as a main course.

2

Mushrooms: Not your Ordinary Vegetable or Plant

One of the most unique foods that we consume on a regular basis is mushrooms. Unlike any ordinary vegetable or plant, mushrooms are actually members of the fungus family. They are produced from spores rather than seeds, and therefore lack the familiar plant traits of leaves, flowers, and roots.

During the development of normal plants, nutrition is absorbed by not only the roots system, but also by the presence of chlorophyll in the green leaves and stems. Mushrooms on the other hand must find other ways to derive nutrition to aid in their maturation. In order to do this, they adhere themselves to different organic matters and feed on the nutritional elements that are naturally found there.

Although there are thousands of different varieties of mushrooms, less than twenty species are cultivated commercially. The most standard varieties that we find in the retail markets here in the Fraser Valley are the white button (common mushroom), shitake, portabella, oyster, and occasionally enoki mushrooms.

White button are the most commonly used mushrooms that we are all most familiar with. Therefore they are the most recognizable mushroom and the most widely cultivated variety. Shitake mushrooms originated in Asia. They are dark brown, have a smoky and somewhat nutty flavor, and the tough woody stems are usually discarded. Portabellas are very large with their tops ranging anywhere from

7 to 12 centimetres and are known as the steak of all mushrooms. Oyster mushrooms are fluted and their stems are usually grouped together. They have a mild flavour that some say is reminiscent of oysters. Enoki mushrooms are the smallest and most delicate of the varieties listed here. They grow in clusters of small white caps on long thin stems that are usually 6 to 10 centimetres long.

Occasionally mushrooms are served as the principal component of a dish, such as stuffed mushrooms, however they are usually added to a recipe as one of the ingredients or accompaniments, such as in soups, salads, omelets, and pizzas for example. They are available not only fresh, but also dried and canned as well. If you are buying dried mushrooms, re-hydrate for approximately 30 minutes in just enough warm water to cover them, and reserve the flavored residual liquid to add to recipes along with the refreshed mushrooms themselves. Canned mushrooms are usually just the ones of the white common variety and come in whole, slices, or pieces. Despite being convenient, canned mushrooms lack the same nutritional value as fresh mushrooms due to the processing procedures involved. They also have a completely different flavour and texture than fresh as well.

Although fresh mushrooms don't keep well for long periods of time, the ideal storing environment is in the refrigerator in a brown paper bag, rather than in plastic. This allows for proper air circulation by letting the mushrooms "breathe". Trapping moisture in a plastic produce bag will cause rapid deterioration and the development of bacteria. Mushrooms consist of mostly water and therefore can spoil very quickly if not kept in the proper environment.

Many non-cultivated wild mushrooms can be very poisonous, and even lethal. To be safe, you should always avoid eating any wild mushrooms unless you are professionally trained to recognize the different varieties that naturally grow in the wild.

Dear Chef Dez:
What is the best way to clean mushrooms? Should I wash them like any other vegetable that I buy at the store?

Shirley G.
Mission, BC

Dear Shirley:
The best way to clean mushrooms for cooking is simply by rubbing them with a damp cloth. Washing them in water causes them to be over-soaked and will reduce the amount of natural flavour that they have to offer. If serving them in the raw form, some people prefer to quickly rinse them under cold water, and this can be fine as long as they are not soaked in water. Additionally, you can add a bit of white vinegar to this rinsing water to help keep raw button mushrooms looking as white as possible.

Coq au Vin

Full colour photo available at www.chefdez.com

"Don't be intimidated by the fancy French name. It is simply pronounced, "coke oh van" and loosely translated is "chicken in wine", or more precisely "rooster in wine.""

1/3 (one third) cup flour, seasoned with salt & pepper
4 chicken thighs
3 thick bacon slices, cut into ¼ (one quarter) inch pieces
10 medium to large mushrooms, quartered
12 pearl onions, peeled and left whole
2 - 3 garlic cloves, crushed
1 tsp dried thyme leaves
1 cup and a splash of Pinot Noir or other red wine
2 bay leaves
Salt & fresh cracked pepper, to taste
1 - 2 tsp butter (optional)
Fresh chopped parsley and fresh thyme for garnish (optional)

1. Heat heavy bottomed pan over medium heat.
2. Dredge chicken in the seasoned flour.
3. Add the bacon to the pan and render it until almost crisp; remove with a slotted spoon and set aside.
4. Turn the heat to medium-high and brown the chicken pieces in the bacon fat on both sides; approximately 6 minutes total - Remove the chicken and set aside with the bacon pieces.
5. Lower heat to medium and add the mushrooms, onions, garlic and thyme; sauté for approximately 2 or 3 minutes until softened a bit. Then deglaze the pan (loosen the browned bits cooked on the pan) with a splash of Pinot Noir and a wooden spoon.
6. Add the bacon, chicken, 1 cup Pinot Noir, and bay leaves; bring to a boil over medium-high heat. Once boiling, turn down to simmer; cover and cook for 30-35 minutes until the chicken is cooked through.
7. Remove the chicken thighs, onions, mushrooms, and bacon with a slotted spoon and set aside covered with foil to keep warm. Discard the Bay leaves.
8. Increase the heat to medium-high and reduce the liquid by about half, approximately 5 minutes. Taste and adjust the seasonings with salt and fresh

cracked pepper after it has reduced.

9 Finish the sauce by removing the pan from the heat and stirring in the butter until just melted (optional).

10 Serve immediately: plate each chicken thigh with 3 onions, 10 mushroom quarters, a few bacon pieces, and drizzle a couple tablespoons of sauce over and around chicken.

11 If desired, garnish with fresh chopped parsley, and a sprig of fresh thyme.

Makes 4 portions

Marinated & Grilled Portabellas

"Who would have ever thought that a mushroom could have this much flavour!"

¼ (one quarter) cup olive oil
¼ (one quarter) cup balsamic vinegar
2 tsp dried oregano leaves
1 tsp dried basil leaves
1 tsp sugar
½ (one half) tsp salt
¼ (one half) tsp fresh cracked pepper
2 large portabella mushrooms

1 Whisk all the ingredients (except for the mushrooms) together in a small bowl.

2 Place the mushrooms and marinade in a plastic bag, ensuring it is sealed.

3 Gently handle the bag back and forth to coat the mushrooms.

4 Marinate in the refrigerator for 2 to 24 hours. Flip the bag once or twice during this time period to allow for more even flavour saturation.

5 Remove the mushrooms from the marinade and grill them on a hot barbeque until slightly charred and cooked through, approximately 3 – 5 minutes per side.

Serves 2

Serving Suggestions

Use in place of a hamburger patties. Serve on buns with a variety of toppings like roasted garlic mayonnaise, melted cheese, lettuce, tomato, etc.

Turn your ordinary eggs benedict into something completely different. Use one of these portabellas as a replacement for the English muffin for a low carbohydrate experience.

Slice them and use to top a variety of dishes like steaks & salads, or add to pasta dishes.

Mushroom Omelet

Full colour photo available at www.chefdez.com

"It is important to use strong cheddar as it really adds tons of flavour. An omelet has never looked or tasted this good before!"

4 or 5 large button mushrooms, thinly sliced
Olive oil
1 tbsp chopped onion
1 clove garlic chopped
2 eggs room temperature
1 tbsp water
Salt and Pepper
¾ (three quarters) cup grated old cheddar, loosely packed
Chopped fresh parsley

1 Reserve four slices of mushrooms.
2 Put the remainder of the mushrooms in a pan with 1 tbsp olive oil. Season with salt and pepper and cook over medium/high heat, stirring occasionally, until the liquid has evaporated and they have browned. Remove from heat and set aside.
3 In a separate small nonstick frying pan over medium heat add 1 tsp olive oil. When the pan is warm add the four slices of raw mushrooms (from step 1), onion and garlic. Season with salt and pepper and cook until soft; approximately 1 to 2 minutes, stirring occasionally.

4 In a small bowl, beat eggs with water. Add to the onion, garlic, mushrooms in the small pan.

5 When the eggs begin to set around the edges use a heat resistant silicone spatula to loosen edges. Turn the pan while lifting the omelet to allow uncooked egg mixture to seep under the cooked egg.

6 Once almost fully set, turn heat to low and season with salt and pepper.

7 Place ¼ cup of the cheese on half of the open omelet. Put ¾ of the sautéed mushrooms (from step 2) on top of the cheese and put another ¼ cup of cheese on top of the mushrooms.

8 With the silicone spatula fold the uncovered half of the omelet over the mushroom cheese mixture.

9 Layer on top of the omelet with half of the remaining cheese and then all of the remaining mushrooms and then the balance of the cheese. Leave omelet in the pan over low heat until the cheese on top is almost melted.

10 Carefully slide the omelet with the spatula onto a plate. Garnish with chopped parsley and enjoy!

Makes one omelet.

Mushroom Salad with Spicy Bacon Dressing

"Use any mixture of mushrooms that are available at your market - what I have listed here is my recommendation"

SALAD

600g white button mushrooms, quartered

200g shitake mushrooms, stems removed & quartered

200g portabella mushrooms, roughly chopped

1 medium carrot, peeled & grated

1 green bell pepper, diced small

1 red bell pepper, diced small

4 green onions, sliced

1 handful fresh parsley, minced

DRESSING

250g bacon slices, cooked crisp, drained and fat reserved
5 tbsp apple cider vinegar
3 tbsp Dijon mustard
5 tsp sambal oelek
2 tsp liquid honey
2 tsp anchovy paste, or two anchovies
1 garlic clove, crushed
1 tsp salt
½ (one half) tsp fresh cracked pepper
1 cup olive oil

1. Place all the salad ingredients in a large mixing bowl.
2. In a food processor, process the crisp bacon into fine bits, approximately 30 seconds on high.
3. Scrape down the sides of the food processor. Add 2 tablespoons of the reserved bacon fat and the remaining dressing ingredients except for the olive oil.
4. Turn the processor on high and drizzle the olive oil slowly into the moving mixture. Once the oil has been added, continue to puree on high for approximately 30 seconds to one minute.
5. Toss the dressing thoroughly into the salad ingredients and serve.

Makes 6 – 10 portions as a side dish

Pastry Wrapped Wild Mushroom Halibut

"If fresh halibut filets are not available, use frozen – just thaw and pat them dry with paper towel."

2 tbsp butter
½ (one half) medium onion, diced small
6 garlic cloves, minced
Salt & pepper
1 pound mixed variety of mushrooms, sliced
- Preferably portabella, shitake, & oyster mushrooms
¼ (one quarter) cup white wine

½ (one half) cup whipping cream

1 tsp sugar

2 pounds fresh, boneless halibut filets

2 – 397g pkgs of frozen puff pastry, thawed & chilled

All purpose flour

1 egg, mixed with 1 tbsp water

Fresh chives

1 lemon

1. Preheat oven to 400 degrees.
2. Over medium heat, melt butter in a large non-stick pan.
3. Add the onions, garlic, and season with salt & pepper. Cook until soft, approximately 2 – 3 minutes, stirring occasionally.
4. Add the sliced mushrooms and the white wine. Season with more salt & pepper. Turn the heat to medium-high and cook until soft, approximately 3 minutes, stirring occasionally.
5. Stir in the whipping cream and sugar. Taste & re-season if necessary, and remove from the heat.
6. Cut the fish into 6 equal portions and lightly season both sides with salt & pepper.
7. Cut pastry into 6 equal portions. On a lightly floured surface, roll out pastry portions into rectangles large enough to enclose each piece of fish.
8. Place each piece of fish on a portion of pastry, and top each one with 1/6 of the mushroom mixture, approximately 3 – 4 tablespoons. Add 2 sprigs of chives, chopped to each portion.
9. With a pastry brush, moisten all of the edges of the pastry with egg wash. Enclose each portion by folding up the sides and tucking underneath to completely enclose the halibut pieces.
10. Place pastry packets on a parchment paper lined baking sheet and bake for 25 minutes until golden brown.
11. Garnish each portion with a twist of lemon and chopped fresh chives.

Makes 6 portions

Tomato Mushroom Rosé Pasta Sauce

Full colour photo available at www.chefdez.com

"Thick slices of the mushrooms will make them very prominent in this recipe"

1 small to medium carrot, diced very small
1 large celery stalk, diced very small
½ (one half) medium white onion, diced very small
6 cloves of garlic, crushed
4 tbsp olive oil
20 medium to large button mushrooms, thick sliced
28 fl oz. can of diced tomatoes
1 cup Merlot or other full-bodied red wine
1 tbsp & 1 tsp white sugar
¼ (one quarter) cup 35% whipping cream
Salt & fresh cracked pepper to taste
Freshly cooked pasta
Fresh chopped parsley & Parmesan cheese, optional

1. Heat heavy bottomed pot over medium heat.
2. Add 2 of the tablespoons of olive oil, carrot, celery, onion, and garlic. Gently season with salt & pepper, and sweat until soft but not brown, about 2 – 3 minutes; stirring frequently.
3. Add mushrooms, the other 2 tablespoons of olive oil, and a sprinkle of salt; gently cook for about 2 – 3 minutes stirring occasionally.
4. Add can of tomatoes (not drained).
5. Turn heat to high and reduce until liquid almost gone; watching closely and stirring frequently while gradually lowering heat from high to medium-high; about 10 – 15 minutes.
6. Add the Merlot and reduce again over medium-high heat; stirring occasionally while gradually lowering heat to medium; about 10 minutes. Stir in the sugar.
7. Stir in the cream and remove from heat. Season to taste.
8. Serve with your favorite pasta and garnish with freshly chopped parsley and grated Parmesan cheese.

Makes 4 to 6 portions on the amount of pasta

Wild Mushroom Risotto

"Arborio rice is the classic rice used in risotto – it becomes very creamy as it is stirred and the liquids are absorbed. A delicious side dish – well worth the effort!"

5 cups chicken broth
4 tbsp olive oil
1 medium sized shallot, minced
3 garlic cloves, minced
1 pound mixed variety of mushrooms, sliced
½ (one half) tsp salt
2 cups Arborio rice
1 cup white wine
½ (one half) cup grated asiago cheese
Salt & fresh cracked pepper to taste

1 Simmer the chicken broth in a small pot.
2 Heat a separate heavy bottomed pot over medium heat. Add 2 tbsp of the olive oil, and sauté the shallot and garlic briefly (about 1 minute) stirring frequently.
3 Add the mushrooms, the other 2 tbsp of oil, and the salt – cook, stirring occasionally, until the mushrooms reduce in volume slightly; about 2 or 3 minutes.
4 Add the dry rice and cook for about 3 or 4 minutes until rice starts to look opaque, stirring frequently.
5 Add the white wine and cook until all the liquid is almost gone, stirring constantly.
6 Start ladling warm chicken broth one ladle at a time until each one is almost absorbed, before adding the next ladle. Keep doing this until all the broth has been absorbed (about 15 to 20 minutes) stirring constantly.
7 Remove the pot from the heat, and stir in the grated cheese.
8 Season to taste with salt and fresh cracked pepper and serve immediately.

Makes 4 to 6 portions

3
Parsley is not just Garnish on your Plate

There are many Chefs that ridicule the idea of using parsley as a garnish on a plate. They argue that it has just been used too much in the past and they are always challenging themselves to garnish with everything except parsley. I, on the other hand, think it's an affordable way for many people to beautify the meals that they serve. I'm not referring to just having a lonely little sprig on the side of the plate, but having chopped parsley in a splash of vibrant green sprinkled over the dish. At that point you can combine with other garnishes as well, if so desired.

I am constantly preaching to my Culinary Students that the "eyes always eat first". This means that one will always assume that a meal is fabulous, before even tasting it, if it is garnished beautifully! However, parsley is not used just for garnish.

Parsley is botanically called *petroselinum crispum*. This is derived from the Greek word *petros*, meaning stone, as it was often found growing in and around groups of rocks. Today this herb, naturally high in vitamin A and C, is usually available in just two different varieties. Curly leaf parsley is the most common one we see today at the local grocery store, however in some markets, flat leaf Italian parsley is just as common. The main visual difference between the two is just what the names predict, however flat leaf Italian parsley has more flavour than its curly common counterpart.

When parsley is being used for purposes other than garnish, it is usually added as a minor ingredient to characterize a dish with a distinct touch of natural herb flavour and a bit of colour. When doing so, make sure it is added closer to the end of the cooking time, as with most fresh herbs, because of the dramatic loss of flavour if it is cooked too long.

However, there are some recipes that use parsley as a main ingredient. Salsa Verde for example, is a sauce that mainly consists of fresh parsley ground with an array of ingredients such as capers, garlic, anchovies, etc. It is a great sauce for almost any application – on grilled meats & fish, potatoes, steamed vegetables, and even sandwiches. Another great sauce is pesto. Traditionally pesto is prepared by pureeing fresh basil leaves mainly with olive oil, pine nuts, garlic, parmesan cheese, and lemon juice to form an outstanding pasta sauce, however the basil leaves can be substituted with parsley. This makes the pesto recipe not only more affordable, but also easier to create from scratch all year round, as fresh parsley is more accessible in the markets than fresh basil.

You can purchase parsley in two different forms: fresh or dried. I obviously recommend buying fresh, as the dried variety lacks flavour, colour, and nutritional value in comparison. If you find it difficult to discover enough ways to use up a whole "bunch" of fresh parsley before it wilts or starts to spoil, it can be frozen. To prepare it for freezing, it should be washed and dried completely (I recommend a salad spinner), stems removed, chopped small, and laid out on a parchment or wax paper covered baking sheet. Place this in the freezer for a couple of hours and then slide the frozen individualized pieces into a freezer bag. Store this bag in your freezer, and conveniently withdraw a handful of parsley whenever it is needed. Due to its minuscule size it does not have to be thawed before using, as the warmth of the dish or the temperature of the room will do this efficiently enough.

Dear Chef Dez:
I hate wasting food. I usually put my parsley stems in my garden composter with all my other vegetable trimmings, but I was wondering if there are any uses for them?
Bonnie S.
Abbotsford, BC

Dear Bonnie:
Parsley stems are a great way to add flavour to homemade chicken broth. Simply add the parsley stems at the same time as all the other aromatics. If the making of homemade broth is an infrequent event in your kitchen, then collect your washed parsley stems in a freezer bag, and keep them frozen until needed.
Alternatively, I have seen a recipe utilizing "fried stalks" as a side dish. Conveniently just toss the fresh stalks into a pan and sauté with a bit of olive oil (or butter), crushed garlic, and seasonings.

Linguine Puttanesca

Full colour photo available at www.chefdez.com

"Linguine Puttanesca (pronounced "ling-gweenee poo-tan-ness-ka") is a classic dish from old world Italy. Rumors indicates that Italian "working women" created this dish as a quick meal to prepare between visits with clients."

2 – 3 tbsp olive oil
1 tsp dried crushed chilies
2 cloves garlic, minced
2 tsp anchovy paste, or 2 anchovy filets
1 – 796ml can of diced tomatoes, drained
2 tbsp red or white wine (optional)
½ (one half) cup pitted & halved kalamata olives, firmly packed
2 tbsp capers, drained
¾ (three quarter) cup chopped fresh parsley, loosely packed
300g dry linguine, cooked al denté
Salt & fresh cracked pepper to season

1 Add the oil, chilies, garlic and anchovy to a large pan and heat over medium-low heat to infuse the flavours – approximately 3 to 5 minutes. Be careful not to burn the garlic.

2 Add the drained tomatoes and the wine (optional) and increase the heat to medium-high. Boil until reduced – approximately 4 to 5 minutes. Stirring occasionally.

3 Remove from the heat. Toss in the olives, capers, parsley and hot cooked pasta.

4 Season to taste with salt and pepper and serve immediately.

Makes approximately 4 portions

Parsley Pesto

Full colour photo available at www.chefdez.com

"Pesto is traditionally made with basil, but parsley is more readily available and works extremely well in this recipe!"

2/3 (two thirds) cup roasted, salted cashews
½ (one half) cup extra virgin olive oil
½ (one half) cup grated Parmesan cheese
2 large garlic cloves, peeled
Juice of a ½ (one half) lemon
½ (one half) tsp salt
½ (one half) tsp fresh cracked pepper
1 bunch fresh curly leaf parsley, large stems removed

1. In a food processor, grind the cashews on high speed for approximately 15 seconds.
2. Continue to process on high speed while slowly adding ¼ (one quarter) cup of the olive oil through the top opening, and then process for another 30 seconds until mixture is almost completely smooth and liquid.
3. Turn off the processor. Add the cheese, garlic, lemon juice, salt, and pepper. Turn the processor back on and process on high speed while feeding the parsley through the top opening. When all of the parsley has been added, continue to process on high speed while slowly adding the remaining ¼ (one quarter) cup of olive oil.
4. Turn off the processor, scrape down the sides, and process for another 10 to 15 seconds.
5. Toss with hot freshly cooked pasta of your choice, or use in a variety applications such as a pizza or bruscetta topping."

Makes approximately 1 ½ (one and one half) cups – enough for 2 large pasta portions.

Salsa Verde

"Great on sandwiches, bruscetta, grilled chicken breast, grilled fish, or served with a cheese & cracker platter"

1 slice bread
¼ (one quarter) cup sun-dried tomatoes, packed in oil, drained
1 large garlic clove, peeled
1 bunch fresh parsley, large stems removed
Zest of 1 lime, finely chopped
Juice from ½ lime
5 tbsp extra-virgin olive oil
1 tbsp capers, drained
1 tsp anchovy paste, or 1 anchovy filet
1 tsp sugar
½ (one half) tsp salt
½ (one half) tsp fresh cracked pepper
¼ (one quarter) tsp sambal oelek

1. In a food processor, process the bread slice on high speed until fine crumbs are formed, approximately 15 to 30 seconds.
2. Add all of the remaining ingredients to the bread crumbs and process on high for approximately 30 seconds. Scrape down the sides of the processor, and process for another 30 seconds until smooth texture is formed.

Makes approximately 1 cup

Scampi

Full colour photo available at www.chefdez.com

"Great as an appetizer, main course, or a side dish to a seafood feast!"

½ (one half) cup extra virgin olive oil
1 head (10 – 12 cloves) garlic, minced
680g (1.5 pounds) large prawns, peeled & de-veined, tail-on

1 cup finely chopped fresh parsley
Juice of ½ lemon
Salt & pepper
Extra lemon wedges for serving

1. Place the oil and garlic in a large non-stick pan. Turn the heat to medium-low and heat to infuse the oil with garlic flavour, approximately 15 minutes. Be careful not to burn the garlic – you may need to lower the heat halfway through the 15 minutes.
2. Add the prawns and increase the heat to medium-high. Cook just until they have turned pink, tossing frequently – DO NOT OVER COOK.
3. Remove from the heat. Stir in the parsley and lemon juice. Season to taste with salt and pepper.
4. Serve immediately, spooning the oil "sauce" over the prawns.

Makes 4 portions as an appetizer and 2 as a main course

CHEF DEZ

4

Is it Mr. Eggplant or Mrs. Eggplant?

While shopping amongst all the wonderful produce our stores have to offer, how many of you pass up the opportunity of putting a couple of eggplants in your basket? This wonderful fruit, more often than not, stays in the produce bin rather than making it to one's family dinner table. There seem to be countless people that do not know enough about them, so hopefully I can shed some light for you.

Eggplant, as mentioned above, is technically a fruit not a vegetable. There are common characteristic differences between fruit and vegetables. Fruit is usually the product of a plant or tree and contains seeds or a pit, while vegetables are the stalks, roots, and leaves of the plants themselves. Allow me to give you a couple of examples: apples are obviously fruit – they are a product of a plant and have seeds. Broccoli is a vegetable as it is the stalk of a plant. Oranges, peaches, grapefruit, lemons, grapes, etc. are all fruit, while onions, carrots, asparagus, lettuce, etc. are all vegetables. Today's consumer most commonly differentiates fruits from vegetables on the basis of sweetness or lack thereof. Although determination by judging sweetness would be generally correct, it would eliminate such fruits as tomatoes, peppers, avocados, and eggplants.

There are many types of eggplants that are cultivated around the world. The variety of eggplant that is most common in our markets is the pear-shaped deep purple coloured species, and is appropriately named the "common eggplant". Therefore I will focus on them specifically.

Eggplants have a spongy flesh with a mild yet sometimes bitter flavour. Many prefer to peel eggplants, however the skin is completely edible. When choosing one at the produce counter, make sure that the skin is unblemished and it is uniform in coulour and shape. The small edible seeds that are inside the eggplants are the culprits for causing most of the bitter flavour they may have. Therefore, select one that has fewer seeds. The best way to go about doing this, other than cutting one open, is by choosing a male eggplant over a female one. Refraining from going deep into plant horticulture, I will simply say that there are male and female differences. Detecting these differences in eggplant is not as difficult as it may seem. Male eggplants are usually more rounded on the lower half of the pear-shape and have a smoother bottom where the flower base is located. Female eggplants have a more slender pear-shape and you can feel that the bottom flower base at the bottom of the eggplant is indented. You will find in comparison that the male eggplant will usually have less seeds than the female.

Regardless of which eggplant you may have purchased, there are other ways to remove some of the bitter flavour. Simply salt slices of the eggplant and let drain for 1 to 2 hours. Although this is effective for removing bitterness, it also obviously removes a lot of the water content as well. So therefore, this step may work better with some recipes more than others.

There are many great dishes that you can prepare with eggplant. They can be halved, stuffed, grilled, and baked. Stew them with tomatoes and other vegetables to make a "ratatouille", or use slices to replace the pasta for a lower carbohydrate lasagna. Or try making Greek moussaka - a very delicious casserole made with eggplant, ground lamb and cream sauce.

Dear Chef Dez:
I tried pan-frying cubes of eggplant for a recipe, and they sucked up all the oil I had in the pan. Is this normal, and if not, how can I prevent this from happening?
Angie D.
Abbotsford, BC

Dear Angie:
Yes, this is completely normal. The great thing about this is that it soaks up flavour at the same time! Since eggplants are very mild, this makes for an excellent opportunity to add some flavour to them. If you did want to avoid soaking up as much oil, you could accomplish this by coating the eggplant with flour, beaten eggs, and a breading before pan-frying (if the recipe allows for this). A vegetable based oil spray in the pan works great as well.

Creamy Stuffed Eggplant

Full colour photo available at www.chefdez.com

"Even people who don't care for eggplant will find this recipe appealing"

1 large eggplant
1 tbsp + 2 tsp olive oil
Salt and pepper
1 tbsp butter
8 medium mushrooms, finely chopped
4 garlic cloves, minced
1 small onion, finely chopped
1 tsp salt
½ (one half) tsp fresh cracked pepper
1 cup cream cheese
6 tbsp grated Parmesan cheese
1 – 170g can crabmeat, drained

1. Preheat oven to 350 degrees.
2. Cut the eggplant in half lengthwise and hollow out halves with a melon baller, leaving approximately ¼ (one quarter) inch thickness around the sides, and ½ (one half) inch thickness on the bottom. Reserve the removed innards.
3. Drizzle 1 tsp of olive oil on each of the hollowed out exposed eggplant halves. Season with salt and pepper and bake on a baking sheet until tender, approximately 20 minutes.
4. Roughly chop the eggplant innards.
5. Add the 1 tbsp olive oil and butter to a large nonstick pan over medium heat. Once the butter is melted, add the chopped eggplant innards, mushrooms, garlic, onion, salt and pepper. Cook until all vegetables are soft and the liquid has evaporated, approximately 7 to 10 minutes, stirring occasionally.
6. Stir in the cream cheese and 4 tbsp of the Parmesan cheese. Once fully combined remove from the heat and stir in the crabmeat. Season to taste.
7. Fill the two eggplant halves equally with the stuffing. Sprinkle the remaining two tbsp of Parmesan cheese over the stuffed eggplants.
8. Place under the broiler until golden brown, approximately 2 to 5 minutes depending on how close they are to the broiler.
9. Serve immediately, cutting each half into thirds to make 6 portions.

Makes 6 portions as a side dish.

Moussaka

"Greek eggplant lasagna at its best! The cinnamon, cloves and nutmeg compliment this dish with earthy aromas and flavours."

EGGPLANT LAYERS

3 large eggplants, cut into ½ (one half) inch slices
Salt
Olive oil

MEAT SAUCE LAYERS

1½ (one and one half) lbs lean ground beef
1 medium onion, diced small
6 cloves garlic minced
2 tsp oregano
1 tsp thyme
½ (one half) tsp cinnamon
¼ (one quarter) tsp cloves
Pinch of nutmeg
Salt and pepper
1-156ml can tomato paste
1 cup full-bodied red wine
½ (one half) cup canned beef broth (undiluted)
1 tbsp sugar

BÉCHAMEL SAUCE LAYER

5 tbsp butter
6 tbsp flour
3 cups milk
1 medium onion peeled and halved
8 whole cloves
150g feta cheese, crumbled finely
Salt and white pepper
¼ (one quarter) cup grated
Parmesan cheese

1 Salt the eggplant slices and lay them in a colander to drain for 1 hour.
2 Rinse the eggplants and pat them dry.
3 Pre-heat heavy bottomed pan over medium to medium-high heat.
4 Fry eggplant slices in minimal amount of oil, on both sides until browned. Add olive oil as necessary in minimal amounts. Set the eggplant slices aside when cooked.

MEAT SAUCE

5 Lower the heat for the pan to medium.
6 Add ground beef, onion, garlic, oregano, thyme, cinnamon, cloves, nutmeg, salt and pepper to the pan. Cook until browned; approximately ten minutes, stirring occasionally.

7 Stir tomato paste into ground beef.

8 Add wine, beef broth and sugar. Bring to a boil and reduce until thickened.

9 Taste and re-season with salt and pepper if necessary. Remove from heat and set aside.

BÉCHAMEL

10 In a heavy bottomed saucepan melt the butter over low heat and add flour. Cook for approximately 2 to 3 minutes to remove starchy flavour.

11 Pour milk into a microwave safe container

12 Stud the cut onion with whole cloves. Submerse onion in milk and microwave until hot.

13 Remove the onion and cloves from the milk.

14 With heat on low, add the milk slowly into the butter/flower mixture while whisking constantly.

15 When all of the milk has been incorporated, increase heat to medium to bring mixture to a boil while whisking constantly. (Sauce will not be fully thickened until it has reached the boiling point.) Remove from heat.

16 Stir in the feta cheese to the béchamel sauce. (Cheese will not fully melt.) Taste and season with salt and white pepper.

Assembly

Pre-heat oven to 350 degrees
Grease a deep 9 x 13 inch baking dish.
Separate eggplant into three equal amounts for the layers.
Arrange one layer of eggplant at the bottom of the pan, cutting when necessary to make them fit. Spread one half of the meat sauce over the eggplant. Arrange the second layer of eggplant over the sauce. Spread on remaining meat sauce. Arrange last layer of eggplant and top with béchamel. Sprinkle with Parmesan cheese. Bake for approximately 35 minutes until the top is golden brown.
Remove from oven and let it rest for approximately 10 – 20 minutes before serving.

Makes 10 – 12 portions

Ratatouille

"A classic vegetable side dish of cubed vegetables tossed in basil infused tomato sauce"

3 tbsp extra virgin olive oil
1 small sized eggplant, ½ (one half)inch cubes
1 small red onion, ½ (one half) inch dice
6 mushrooms, halved or quartered
1 small zucchini, ½ (one half) inch cubes
1 yellow bell pepper, ½ (one half) inch dice
4 large garlic cloves, minced
2 tsp dried thyme leaves
Salt & pepper
1 – 796ml can diced tomatoes, not drained
1 – 156ml can tomato paste
2 tbsp sugar
1 large handful fresh basil leaves, sliced thin *See notes following

1. Preheat a large nonstick pan over medium heat. Once hot add the olive oil.
2. Add the eggplant, onion, mushrooms, zucchini, bell pepper, garlic, thyme, and season generously with salt and pepper. Sauté for 4 to 5 minutes until vegetables are softened a bit, stirring occasionally.
3. Turn the heat to medium-high and stir in the tomatoes, tomato paste and sugar. Continue to cook until the vegetables are thoroughly cooked and a thick tomato sauce forms, approximately 6 to 8 minutes, stirring occasionally.
4. Remove from the heat. Stir in the fresh basil, season to taste with salt and pepper, and serve immediately.

Makes 4 to 6 portions as a side vegetable dish – also great served on pasta.

Basil notes:

- To slice the fresh basil leaves, stack the leaves and roll them into a cigar shape before slicing – it will minimize your efforts by making more cuts with each pass of the knife. Fresh basil bruises easily and this will also minimize the damage to the basil.
- If fresh basil is not available, use 3 tbsp dried basil leaves (not ground) and add it at the same time as the dried thyme leaves.

Stacked Eggplant Appy

Full colour photo available at www.chefdez.com (PICTURED ON FRONT COVER)

"The crumbled goat cheese adds a lot of richness to the taste of the eggplant, and is a great contrast to the corn & date salsa"

1 large eggplant
4 tbsp olive oil
salt & pepper
2 large red bell peppers
100g soft unripened goat cheese

CORN & DATE SALSA TOPPING

1 - 341ml can whole kernel corn, drained well
Trimmings from bell peppers (above)
2/3 (two thirds) packed cup of loose dates, finely chopped
1 large jalapeno pepper, diced small, seeds and inner membrane removed
¼ (one quarter) cup finely chopped red onion
1 garlic clove, crushed
1 tbsp balsamic vinegar
¼ (one quarter) tsp salt
Pinch of fresh cracked pepper

1. Preheat oven to 450 degrees.
2. Cut the eggplant into 6, ½ (one half) inch thick rounds. Toss with 2 tbsp of the olive oil. Season both sides of the rounds with salt and pepper and place them on a large baking sheet.
3. Cut the sides and bottoms off the bell peppers (reserving the top trimmings for the salsa). Toss the sides and bottoms with the other 2 tbsp olive oil. Place them on the same baking sheet as the eggplant.
4. Bake the eggplant and the bell peppers in the oven for 10 minutes. Remove from the oven to flip the peppers and carefully flip the eggplant over. Return to the oven and bake for another 5 minutes. Remove from the oven.
5. Let the eggplant rounds cool to room temperature, meanwhile place the baked red peppers in an air-tight covered glass bowl for at least 10 minutes to loosen the skins. Remove the peppers from the bowl and peel off the skins.
6. While the eggplant and peppers are baking and cooling, cut the leftover red

peppers trimmings into small ¼ inch pieces and add to a medium sized mixing bowl.

7 Add the corn, dates, jalapeno, red onion, garlic, balsamic, salt and pepper to the red pepper trimmings in the bowl. Toss to combine and season to taste, if desired.

Assembly

Plate 1 eggplant round per portion. Top each round with enough roasted bell pepper to cover. Divide the goat cheese into 6 equal parts and crumble over each portion. Top each portion with a desired amount of salsa.

Makes 6 portions

5

The Strawberry Festival is upon us once again!

Strawberry season is one of the most celebrated times of the year for lovers of this luscious red fruit, and thanks to Mother Nature, farmers in the Valley have a "bumper crop"!

Although strawberries seem to be available throughout the entire year, thanks to our friends in California; they are not as good as the ones we get fresh right here from our local farmers. Imported strawberries from warmer climates have been cultivated in a way, which produces a larger and firmer berry more durable for transport. This is great for having strawberries available year-round, however these cultivation methods are also the culprit for producing a berry that usually is not as sweet or flavourful as it's more natural counter-part. Thus we tend to rely on sweeteners and flavour enhancers, such as sugar or chocolate, when serving them. Fresh cracked pepper is also, surprisingly; a great way to bring out the flavour of fresh berries, but obviously does not tend to add to the natural sweetness of the berry. Try this on your next batch of ripe berries!

Strawberries are very perishable and should be handled and stored with care. First of all, never buy a basket of strawberries that contains any spoiled ones. Although it may only be one berry, microscopic mold spores have already been transferred to adjacent berries in the basket. This will lead to the whole basket of fruit deteriorating faster. Since washing and handling of the berries will also increase the rapidness of spoilage, only wash the amount needed and leave the others untouched.

The washing of strawberries should only be done with the whole berry intact. If the green top is removed, you will find that the center is somewhat hollow. This cavity will collect water and dramatically reduce (water down) the amount of flavour. Unwashed leftover berries should be stored in the refrigerator in a covered container to keep their "musty" odor from dispersing throughout. A drain tray in this container would be ideal, as it would aid in air circulation within, by keeping any moisture trapped at the bottom and away from the berries.

Freezing is another option for preservation, however as with most fruit you lose nutrients and quality. Strawberries are high in vitamin C and the most optimal way of maintaining their nutritional value is to leave them whole. Cut strawberries have more surface area, and thus loose nutrients faster. To prepare for freezing, wash the berries intact, pat them dry, remove the green tops, and scatter them on a wax paper lined cookie sheet for them to freeze individually. Once frozen completely, transfer them to a freezer bag and use them within the next six months for best results.

There are many dishes that you can prepare using strawberries. The most traditional are desserts such as strawberry shortcake and chocolate dipped strawberries. However, they also work great as tid-bits on cheese platter, or make them into a salsa to spoon over grilled fish. Many people have never made a salsa out of fruit, but it is very simple and the contrasting flavours are very complimentary to the grilled fish or meat it is being served upon. To accomplish making a great strawberry salsa, just add an assortment of items to small-diced strawberries, such as red onion, yellow bell pepper, jalapeno, cilantro, lime juice, and season with a little salt & pepper. You will be amazed at the results – and since it is strawberry season, the time to experiment is now!

Dear Chef Dez:
I have attempted to make chocolate covered strawberries in the past, but they never turn out the way they should be. When they are bitten into, the hard chocolate coating breaks apart and falls on to the plate instead of staying on the berry. What can I do to prevent this?

Tracey S.
Mission, BC

Dear Tracey:
When you melt the chocolate to dip the strawberries into, also melt butter with it and mix it together to form your chocolate coating. Once your strawberries are dipped, chill them in the refrigerator to set, but bring them almost to room temperature before serving. The butter will soften the coating, just as room temperature butter is softer than room temperature chocolate. Use two ounces of butter for every four ounces of chocolate.

Fresh Strawberry Margaritas

"Adding the strawberries last to the blender will help to ensure that they don't get fully puréed. The joy of using fresh strawberries is having small chunks in your margarita!"

1/3 (one third) to ½ (one half) cup tequila
1 tbsp orange brandy or regular brandy
2 ½ (two and one half) tbsp sugar
¼ (one quarter) tsp salt
3 cups large ice cubes
20 whole strawberries, green tops removed

1 In a large blender add the tequila, brandy, sugar, and salt.
2 Add the ice cubes.
3 Add the strawberries and replace the lid on the blender.
4 Pulse on high speed just until the ice has been crushed enough to allow the strawberries to start reaching the blades at the bottom of the blender.
5 Blend on high speed briefly until the berries are chopped but not pureed smooth. You should be able to feel bits of strawberries when tasting.
6 Serve immediately.

Makes approximately 4 cups

Chocolate Covered Strawberries

Full colour photo available at www.chefdez.com

8 - 12 large strawberries
4 oz. semi-sweet chocolate
4 tbsp butter
1.5 oz white chocolate

1 Rinse the strawberries, leaving on the green tops. Pat them dry thoroughly.
2 Over low to medium-low heat, bring about two inches of water to a light simmer in a double boiler. If you don't have a double boiler, then just use a pot and a stainless steel bowl instead.

3 Melt the semi-sweet chocolate and the butter together in the top of the double boiler (or the stainless steel bowl), stirring occasionally, until completely melted and combined.

4 By gently holding onto the leaves of a strawberry, dip each one into the melted chocolate/butter mixture. Run one side of the berry against the edge of the bowl before taking it out to remove the excess chocolate, and place that side down on a cookie sheet covered with parchment paper.

5 Store the sheet of berries in the refrigerator to solidify the chocolate coating.

6 Melt the white chocolate over the double boiler in a separate bowl, stirring occasionally until completely melted.

7 Take the cooled strawberries out of the refrigerator. Using a teaspoon, splash the white chocolate vigorously in a "back & forth motion" so that thin lines of white chocolate fall upon the strawberries.

8 Refrigerate once again.

9 Let sit at room temperature for about 15 minutes prior to serving.

Makes 8 – 12 strawberries

Strawberries with Cracked Pepper & Vodka

"This may sound odd, but it is a wonderful combination of flavours, and makes a beautiful display on a platter"

24 fresh strawberries, tops removed, sliced
3 tbsp vodka
freshly cracked black pepper
fresh mint sprigs, for garnish

1 Arrange strawberries on a small platter.

2 Drizzle with vodka.

3 Crack the pepper directly onto the berries with a pepper mill.

4 Garnish with the fresh mint sprigs.

Makes 4 – 6 servings

Strawberry Passoire à la Crème

Full colour photo available at www.chefdez.com

"Passoire is French for colander in which this dessert is made"

1 cup cottage cheese
250g package cream cheese, room temperature
1 tsp pure vanilla extract
¼ (one quarter) tsp salt
Zest from 1 lemon, finely chopped
½ (one half) cup icing sugar
1 cup whipping cream
12 strawberries, chopped or sliced
1 tbsp sugar

1 Over a mixing bowl, press the cottage cheese through a fine wire mesh strainer with a spoon, to produce a fine texture.
2 Add the cream cheese, vanilla, salt, and lemon zest to the cottage cheese. Stir to combine thoroughly.
3 Stir in the icing sugar.
4 Whip the cream to stiff peaks and fold into the cheese mixture.
5 Line a 6-inch wire mesh strainer with a slightly damp thin clean kitchen towel or cheesecloth. Make sure it is big enough to have corners/edges hanging over the sides of the strainer.
6 Spoon the mixture onto the towel/cheesecloth in the strainer. Fold over the excess towel over the top of the mixture once filled.
7 Suspend the filled strainer over a bowl to catch any excess liquid, and chill in the refrigerator for 12 to 24 hours to set. It is fine if there is no excess liquid in the bowl – the towel/cheesecloth will be somewhat absorbent.
8 Toss the strawberries with the sugar and let sit for at least 1 hour to macerate (get juices flowing).
9 Unfold the top of the towel/cheesecloth and invert a plate over the strainer. Turn the strainer and plate over to un-mold the dessert onto the plate, removing the strainer and towel/cheesecloth carefully.
10 Garnish with the macerated berries and serve immediately.

Makes 4 – 8 servings

Strawberry Salsa

"A delicious contrast served on grilled chicken or fish"

10 strawberries, diced small, approximately 1 ½ cups
1 medium yellow bell pepper diced small
½ (one half) jalapeno, minced – seeds & membrane removed for a milder salsa
¼ (one quarter) cup small diced red onion
2 – 4 tbsp finely chopped fresh mint
Zest from 1 lime, finely chopped
2 tbsp lime juice
1 ½ (one and one half) tsp sugar
1 tsp fresh cracked black pepper
¼ (one quarter) tsp salt

1 Mix all ingredients together and refrigerate until needed.

Makes approximately 2 cups

6

If Berries are a Festival, then Cherries are a Jubilee!

Summer is a wonderful time of the year when it comes to the abundance of fresh local fruit that is available, and cherries are one of my utmost favourite. I believe that we all have some fond memory from our childhood of eating cherries in the hot summer sun; either raw and fresh by themselves, or in a favorite family dessert.

The part of the world where cherries originated is very difficult to pinpoint, as they have supposedly been in existence since prehistoric times. Today however, cherries are found all over the world. Birds love cherries, and so it is believed that due to their migration habits, they were the factor most contributing to the spread of cherries trees.

We tend to see and consume only one or two varieties of sweet cherries that are sold in our markets and roadside stands. However, there are many different ones that are cultivated around the world. Cherries are divided into two classifications – sweet cherries and sour cherries. There are over 500 varieties of sweet cherries and over 250 varieties of sour cherries worldwide! Three examples of sweet cherries that would be the most familiar to us would be Gean, Bing, and Bigaroon. Gean cherries are the most common. They are either red or black and very sweet. Bing cherries have skins that are usually not as dark and their flesh is substantially more pale, but they tend to be juicer. Bigaroons are somewhat heart-shaped and their firm flesh can either be red or yellow.

When buying cherries, make sure that they are fully ripe. Cherries do not ripen on their own after harvesting. Also make sure to buy cherries that still have their stems attached. Cherries without stems tend to spoil faster as the stem cavity will expose a part of the inner flesh. Cherries can be kept at room temperature, but as with most fruit, they will always deteriorate more slowly if kept in the refrigerator. Store them in a container or bag away from strong smelling foods, as cherries will tend to easily absorb odours, which will intensely affect their flavour. Cherries can be frozen whole or pitted, but freezing will affect their flavour quality and firmness. Frozen cherries will be best used for cooking.

Pitting cherries can be done with either a knife by cutting them in half, or with a cherry/olive pitter. These manual mechanical devices look almost like a pair of hand pliers. One end has a round compartment, which holds the cherry or olive, while the other end is equipped with a "spike" that inserts into the flesh to push the pit through the opposite end.

Cherries Jubilee is probably the most famous cherry recipe. It is recipe that consists of soaking cherries in a cherry liqueur, cooking them in a sugar syrup, and igniting them with brandy. They are boiled down until the sauce thickens, more cherry liqueur can be added at this point, and then served over ice cream or cake.

One of my favorite childhood recipes is one that my Mother made for our family every cherry season. She calls it "cherry soup". It is whole cherries cooked in a sweet, red, cherry broth with curds made out of flour. It may sound odd, but it is very delicious and can be served either hot or chilled!

Dear Chef Dez:
I just recently bought a whole case of cherries because they were on sale for a great price. What are some ideas that I can do with them other than making jam?

Ron S.
Abbotsford, BC

Dear Ron:
There are many great ways to serve cherries. They add a great contrasting colour and flavour to green salads, and are also delicious in custards, sorbets, ice cream, fruit salads, and pies. Black Forest Cake is another famous dessert with cherries. You can also try making cherry wine or macerating them in vodka to make your own cherry liqueur. Try searching the Internet or the library and I am sure you will come up with many great recipes for serving and preserving cherries!

Baked Cherry Rice Pudding

"Arborio rice is the same rice used in risottos – it becomes very creamy. This recipe is best with the reserved cherries from my cherry liqueur recipe"

2 tsp butter
½ (one half) cup Arborio rice
1 cup re-hydrated dried cherries, sliced in half
-or- 1 cup reserved cherries from cherry liqueur recipe
-or- 1 cup fresh pitted cherries, sliced in half
2 – 3 cinnamon sticks, broken in half
1 vanilla bean, split in half lengthwise
-or- 1 tbsp pure vanilla extract
4 cups homogenized milk
1 cup whipping cream
½ (one half) cup sugar
1 tsp salt

1 Preheat oven to 300 degrees.
2 Butter a 2-litre (8 cup) oven-proof casserole dish. Add the rice, cherries, and cinnamon stick. If using the vanilla bean, add it now as well.
3 In a mixing bowl, whisk together the vanilla extract (if not using the vanilla bean), milk, whipping cream, sugar, and salt. Pour oven the rice/cherries in the casserole dish, and stir to combine.
4 Bake for approximately 2 ½ (two and one half) hours, stirring every 20 minutes.
5 Remove the cinnamon sticks and vanilla bean (if used) and let cool slightly before serving. It will thicken more as it cools.

Makes 4 – 6 servings

Cherries Jubilee

"Serve warm or room temperature over cake or ice cream for an intensely flavoured cherry dessert!"

1 pound fresh cherries, pitted
¼ (one quarter) cup cherry liqueur

¾ (three quarters) cup dark brown sugar

3 ½ (three and a half) tbsp fresh lemon juice

2 tsp lemon zest, finely chopped

Pinch of salt

½ (one half) cup amaretto liqueur

1. In a large heavy bottomed pan add all of the ingredients except for the amaretto. Bring to a full boil over medium-high heat.

2. Add the amaretto and carefully ignite with a long match or grill lighter. Shake the pan until the flames subside.

3. Continue to boil and reduce down until syrupy, approximately 8 to 10 minutes.

4. Serve hot or at room temperature over cake or ice cream.

Makes approximately 2 cups as a dessert topping

Mom's Cherry Soup

Full colour photo available at www.chefdez.com

"My Mom used to make this every summer during cherry season when I was a child. It is one of the many great memories I have. When my Mom was a child, my Grandma used to make it for her and her siblings. In those days, my Grandpa would go to town and bring home just one basket of cherries, because that was all that they could afford. Since there were so many kids, one basket of cherries wouldn't go very far. Grandma came up with this recipe of cherry soup so that they would all get their share of the cherries."

1 pound fresh cherries (approx 3 cups), left whole, stems removed

4 cups + 2 tbsp water

1 ¼ (one and one quarter) cup sugar

¾ (three quarters) cup flour

¼ (one quarter) tsp salt

1. Wash the cherries and place them in a medium sized pot. Add the 4 cups water and 1 cup of the sugar. Bring to a boil over medium-high heat.

2. In a bowl, mix the flour, ¼ (one quarter) cup sugar, and salt together. Add the 2 tbsp water and stir with a fork until the flour mixture is moist. Then with your fingers work the flour mixture to make little "flour curds" and set aside.

3. When cherries have come to a boil, add the curds a small handful at a time.

When the curds have all been added, reduce the heat to medium and boil for 5 more minutes, stirring occasionally.

4 Serve hot or at room temperature.

Makes approximately 4 to 6 servings.

Cherry Citrus Liqueur

Full colour photo available at www.chefdez.com

"2 weeks is well worth the wait to enjoy this liqueur"

2 ½ (two and one half) cups dried cherries, sliced in half
2 ½ (two and one half) cups boiling water
Zest from 1 medium orange, removed with a vegetable peeler
3 cups vodka
½ (one half) cup sugar

1 Pour the boiling water over the dried cherries and let steep for 15 to 25 minutes. Strain well and reserve the water.

2 Take ½ (one half) cup of this reserved water and add it to a small pot with the sugar. If there is not enough cherry water left to make ½ (one half) cup, just use tap water. Warm over medium heat just long enough to dissolve the sugar. Store this sugar syrup in a separate sealed container in the refrigerator.

3 Place orange zest and re-hydrated cherries in a clear glass jar with a sealing lid. Add the vodka and seal tight. Let stand for 2 weeks, shaking periodically.

4 At the end of this 2-week period the vodka should be deep cherry red in colour. Strain the cherries and zest from the vodka. Press on the cherries to remove as much of the liqueur as possible.

5 Stir ½ (one half) cup of the sugar syrup (or more, to taste) into the vodka. Store this cherry liqueur in an airtight bottle.

6 The reserved cherries can be kept to use in desserts such as my "Baked Cherry Rice Pudding" in this chapter. Please keep in mind that these cherries are now saturated with vodka and may not be suitable for all members of your family or if you plan to drive. If the cherries are cooked in a dessert the majority of the alcohol will be eliminated, depending on how long the cooking time is.

Makes approximately 3 ½ (three and one half) cups liqueur

7
A Crash Course on Sauce Making

Today's marketplace is saturated with almost every type of bottled or canned sauce imaginable. Homemade sauces, in many households, have taken a "back-seat" to the readymade varieties that seem to fit into our hectic lifestyles. When we think of making sauces from scratch, many people conjure up the image of a thick gelatinous mass from one of our worst school cafeteria nightmares. However, sauces from scratch don't have to be difficult, and can easily be the best part of a dish.

Traditionally, any sauce is usually made up from one of five leading sauces or "mother sauces". These leading sauce categories are Béchamel, Velouté, Brown, Tomato, and Hollandaise.

Don't let any fancy French names scare you. **Béchamel** is merely a white sauce made from adding milk to a white roux (a mixture of fat and flour that has cooked just long enough to eliminate any starchy taste). **Velouté** is made from adding a white stock (such as chicken, veal, or fish) to a white roux. **Brown** sauce is made by adding a brown stock (beef) to a brown roux (fat/flour mixture that has cooked over low heat to intensify color and taste). **Tomato** sauce is a mixture of tomatoes, stock and sometimes a roux, and **Hollandaise** is a mixture of butter and egg yolks.

Although there are techniques and flavourings that also go along with creating any of these base sauces, they are basically the foundations of many corresponding sauces.

For example: a cheese sauce is originated from adding cheese to a béchamel, and a hollandaise sauce with shallots, white wine vinegar, and tarragon is a béarnaise sauce.

Sauce making however, is not always confined within the parameters of these leading sauces. There are many sauces that do not fall into the gamut of these five main categories. Some examples would be pan gravies, reductions, compound butters, and purees.

Pan gravies are just sauces that are made from the drippings from cooked meat or poultry. Extra stock/broth and a thickener are added to extend the flavours and to coat the finished meat product. Meat that is served "au jus" (pronounced "oh zhoo") means that it is served with its natural clear unthickened juices, however extra stock/broth is usually added to ensure there is enough to go around.

Reductions are simply what their name indicates; liquids that are naturally thickened and intensified through the evaporation of water to create a sauce. Some of the best sauces result from letting naturally occurring liquids in a pan to just cook down. Simply season with salt & pepper, and serve.

Many people don't consider compound butters to be a sauce, but when melted, it is a flavourful liquid that enhances a finished dish. The most popular of all flavoured butters in the chef industry is "maître d'hôtel" butter (pronounced "may truh doh tel"). It is solid butter that is traditionally mixed with chopped parsley, lemon juice, and white pepper. It is then rolled into a cylindrical shape and stored in the refrigerator or freezer until needed. This allows one to cut off circles of the butter to melt on top of a finished product, traditionally steak. Endless creations of compound butters can be made however, for many other dishes besides steaks.

Purees also, don't conform in the definition of the five leading sauces. They acquire their thickness from the maceration of a vegetable, fruit, or an array of ingredients, like pesto for example.

The Internet and library are both great resources to get one started on creating a repertoire of sauces of your very own.

> Dear Chef Dez:
> I like making spaghetti tomato sauce, but it always seems to be lacking something, and always too bland. I've tried just adding more salt, but then it just tastes salty. What are some ideas that I can do?
>
> > Robert D.
> > Aldergrove, BC

> Dear Robert:
> Good sauces require depth of flavour. There are many things you can add to create this, but for a tomato pasta sauce I recommend starting with a sautéed seasoned

mixture of extra virgin olive oil, mire poix (celery, onions, and carrots), and lots of fresh garlic. Add the tomatoes with red wine or stock and cook down until the flavours have intensified and the sauce has thickened. Dried herbs can be added at the beginning, while fresh herbs should only be added just prior to finishing. Also, since tomatoes are acidic a couple teaspoons of sugar will help balance everything out. Before serving, make sure to re-season (salt & pepper).

Compound Butters

"Keep these handy in your refrigerator/freezer as a last minute topping for cooked or grilled meats, poultry, fish and vegetables"

Maître D' Hôtel Butter

1 cup butter, room temperature
¼ (one quarter) cup finely chopped parsley
4 tbsp fresh lemon juice
1 tsp finely chopped lemon zest
½ (one half) tsp salt
½ (one half) tsp ground white pepper

Garlic Butter

1 cup butter, room temperature
4 - 6 large garlic cloves, crushed
¼ (one quarter) cup finely chopped parsley
¼ (one quarter) cup grated parmesan cheese

Tequila Lime Chili Butter

1 cup butter, room temperature

2 tbsp chili powder

2 tbsp tequila

1 tbsp fresh lime juice

1 tsp finely chopped lime zest

Instructions for any of the above compound butter recipes

1 Place all the ingredients in the bowl of an electric mixer.

2 Mix at medium speed, gradually increasing to high speed until fully combined, stopping halfway to scrape down the sides of the bowl.

3 Scrape out onto a piece of wax paper. Wrap one end of the wax paper around the butter and roll into a 1 inch cylindrical shape. Try not to handle the butter too much as the warmth of your hands will melt the butter.

4 Once shaped, roll the butter from the wax paper onto a piece of plastic wrap. Wrap completely and finalize the cylindrical shape by twisting the ends of the plastic wrap closed, and twist in the air while grasping both ends of the plastic wrap. It should resemble the shape/form of a sausage. Twist the ends of the plastic wrap to seal.

5 Store in the refrigerator or freezer until needed.

6 To serve as a complimentary sauce/topping, slice a ¼ (one quarter) inch thick circle of the butter and place on hot cooked meats, poultry, fish or vegetables. The heat from the food will cause the butter to melt and cascade over the food.

Each recipe makes approximately 1 cup of compound butter

Dez's Famous 4-Hour Gravy

"Don't be intimidated by the name – it's 4 hours of cooking time, not 4 hours of constant attention! Made from the slow caramelization process of vegetables. If you have a Sunday afternoon to spare, this gravy offers tons of flavour and well worth the effort"

2 medium carrots, sliced into ¼ (one quarter) inch coins
2 celery stalks, sliced ¼ (one quarter) inch
3 tbsp vegetable oil
1 medium onion, sliced thin
¼ (one quarter) cup butter
6 tbsp flour
½ (one half) cup full-bodied red wine
2 cups concentrated canned beef broth, or vegetable broth
1 tsp sugar
½ (one half) tsp salt
¼ (one quarter) tsp pepper

1 Add carrot, celery and 2 tbsp of the vegetable oil to a large heavy bottomed non-stick pan. Toss to coat in the oil and cook over low to medium-low heat for approximately 1.5 hours, stirring occasionally. The carrot and celery will shrink in size, become soft, and just start to caramelize. *DO NOT CROWD THE PAN – It is important to use a large enough pan otherwise the vegetables will just steam in their juices instead of caramelize. The secret is to slowly caramelize the vegetables without burning them.

2 Stir in the onion and the other tbsp of vegetable oil to the carrots and celery and continue to cook, stirring occasionally, for another approximate 1.5 hours – all of the vegetables will become almost all dark brown (caramelized).

3 Add the butter to the vegetables, let it melt, and stir in the flour. Cook for 45 more minutes, stirring occasionally. The flour will become a "nut brown" in colour.

4 Stir in the wine slowly. It will start to get extremely thick. Continue by slowly stirring in the undiluted broth while incorporating to ensure no lumps.

5 Increase the heat to medium or medium-high while stirring to bring to a boil. Boiling will activate the full thickening power of the flour.

6 Strain the mixture through a wire-mesh strainer while pushing as much liquid as possible from the cooked vegetables. Discard the cooked vegetables.

7 Season the gravy with the sugar, salt, and pepper. If it is too thick then add a bit more liquid broth.

Makes approximately 1 ¾ (one and three quarters) cups

Filet of Beef with Mixed Berry Demiglaze

"A steak topped with a sauce made from a mixture of berries – you have to taste it to believe it! It is important for the pan to be hot enough to sear the steaks – this will add flavour to both the meat and the sauce."

4 thick beef tenderloin steaks
2 tbsp olive oil
Salt & pepper
½ (one half) cup & a splash of red wine
2 cups frozen mixed berries (ex: blackberries, blueberries, raspberries)
2 ½ (two and one half) tsp white sugar
2 tsp beef stock paste
1 tsp butter

1 Oil the tenderloins with one tablespoon of the olive oil, and season them with salt and pepper.
2 Heat a heavy bottomed pan over medium heat.
3 Add the other tablespoon of olive oil to the pan and sear the tenderloins for 2 to 3 minutes on each side for medium rare (depending on thickness and temperature).
4 Remove the tenderloins and set aside covered to keep warm.
5 Deglaze the pan (remove the brown bits from the pan into the wine) with the splash of red wine, scraping with a wooden spoon.
6 Add the other ½ (one half) cup of red wine, berries, sugar, and beef paste to the pan, and bring to a boil over medium high heat.
7 Reduce over the same temperature, while breaking up the berries with a spoon as they start to break down, approximately ten minutes. Mash the berries with a potato masher at this point.
8 Strain this sauce through a wire mesh strainer to remove the berry seeds and return the sauce to the pan. Discard the pulp/seeds left in the strainer.
9 Add the tenderloins back to the pan as well, to reheat and coat with the sauce over medium heat.
10 Remove the tenderloins for plating and make sure the sauce is reduced enough that it is thick and syrupy.
11 Remove the sauce from the heat, and melt the teaspoon of butter into the sauce.
12 Drizzle the sauce on and around the tenderloins.

Makes 4 servings

Three Cheese Sauce

"A basic white sauce transformed into a celebration of cheese! For extra depth of flavour, onion and cloves are infused with the milk."

5 tbsp butter
6 tbsp flour
3 cups milk
1 medium onion, peeled and halved
10 whole cloves
100g extra old cheddar, grated
100g blue cheese, crumbled
100g parmesan cheese, grated
½ (one half) tsp salt
¼ (one quarter) tsp ground white pepper
Pinch of ground nutmeg

1 In a heavy bottomed saucepan melt the butter over low heat and add flour. Cook for approximately 2 to 3 minutes to remove starchy flavour, stirring occasionally.
2 Pour milk into a microwave safe container.
3 Stud the cut onion with the whole cloves. Submerse onion in milk and microwave until hot.
4 Remove the onion and cloves from the milk.
5 With heat on low, add the milk very slowly into the butter/flower mixture while whisking constantly. It will get extremely thick but it will slowly thin out as the milk is gradually added. Adding the milk too fast will cause lumps in the final sauce.
6 When all of the milk has been incorporated, add each of three cheeses a little at a time while stirring to incorporate.
7 Increase heat to medium and bring mixture to a boil while whisking constantly (sauce will not be fully thickened until it has reached the boiling point). Remove from heat and season with the salt, pepper, and nutmeg.
8 It is now ready to use in many applications such as over steamed vegetables, on pasta, or use your imagination.

Makes approximately 4 cups

Tomato Rosé Pasta Sauce

Full colour photo available at www.chefdez.com

"With the inclusion of cream, this tomato sauce becomes rich & irresistible"

3 tbsp olive oil
1 medium/large carrot, diced very small
2 large celery stalks, diced very small
1 medium white onion, diced very small
6 cloves of garlic, minced
1 tbsp dried oregano
2 tsp dried basil
Salt & pepper
1 – 156ml can tomato paste
28 fl oz. can of diced tomatoes
1 cup of full-bodied red wine
½ (one half) cup concentrated vegetable broth, or 1 tsp vegetable paste
2 tbsp white sugar
½ (one half) tsp sambal oelek
¾ (three quarters) cup 35% M.F. whipping cream
Salt & fresh cracked pepper to taste
Fresh parsley, for garnish
Grated Parmesan cheese, for garnish

1 Heat a large heavy bottomed pot over medium to medium-high heat.
2 Add the olive oil.
3 Add carrot, celery, onion, garlic, oregano, and basil. Gently season with salt & pepper, and cook until soft but not brown, about 3 to 5 minutes, stirring frequently.
4 Stir in the tomato paste.
5 Stir in the can of tomatoes (not drained), wine, vegetable broth, sugar, and sambal oelek.
6 Bring to a boil and reduce until liquid almost gone; watching closely and stirring frequently; approximately 10 to 15 minutes. Stir in the cream and remove from the heat.
7 Season to taste and serve with your favorite pasta and garnish with freshly chopped parsley and grated Parmesan cheese.

Makes approximately 6 ½ cups

Tomato Pasta Sauce

"Never buy pre-made store bought pasta sauce again. Suitable for freezing - for pasta sauce at a moment's notice."

3 tbsp olive oil
1 medium/large carrot, diced very small
2 large celery stalks, diced very small
1 medium white onion, diced very small
6 cloves of garlic, minced
1 tbsp dried oregano
2 tsp dried basil
Salt & pepper
1 – 156ml can tomato paste
28 fl oz. can of diced tomatoes
1 cup of full-bodied red wine
½ (one half) cup concentrated vegetable broth, or 1 tsp vegetable paste
2 tbsp white sugar
½ (one half) tsp sambal oelek
Salt & fresh cracked pepper to taste
Fresh parsley, for garnish
Grated Parmesan cheese, for garnish

1. Heat a large heavy bottomed pot over medium to medium-high heat.
2. Add the olive oil.
3. Add carrot, celery, onion, garlic, oregano, and basil. Gently season with salt & pepper, and cook until soft but not brown, about 3 to 5 minutes, stirring frequently.
4. Stir in the tomato paste.
5. Stir in the can of tomatoes (not drained), wine, vegetable broth, sugar, and sambal oelek.
6. Bring to a boil. Reduce until desired consistency is reached; stirring occasionally; approximately 5 to 10 minutes.
7. Season to taste and serve with your favorite pasta and garnish with freshly chopped parsley and grated Parmesan cheese.

Makes approximately 6 cups

8

Salad Dressings: Cold Sauces for Your Lettuce

As a sequel to my last column on "sauces", I thought it would be informative to broaden the topic even further. Most don't consider salad dressings to be sauces, however they share the same definition: a flavourful liquid that enhances a finished dish. Salads do not all necessarily share the characteristic of being made out of lettuce; they do however almost always depend upon a dressing of one aspect or another.

Oil & Vinegar is probably the most common homemade dressing. It can be made very simple or quite complex. The most frequent question I get asked, when it comes to making this type of dressing, is "what oil to vinegar ratio should I be using?" Firstly, this depends upon one's tolerance and desire for acidity. I personally prefer a 2:1 ratio of oil to vinegar: meaning two measurements of oil for every one measurement of vinegar. However, a 1:1, 3:1, 4:1, or even a 5:1 ratio can function just as well, depending on one's tastes. Lemon juice can be used with, or in place of, the vinegar if desired. The technique of making a satisfying oil and vinegar dressing will rely more upon the balance of flavours rather than just the ratio used. Different flavourings will either compliment or counteract a ratio, and thus it will have to be tasted and adjusted as needed.

All oil & vinegar dressings are emulsified (mixed together) before serving. They can be either temporarily emulsified or permanently emulsified. A temporary emulsion is when the mixture is shaken and the oil and vinegar is combined together temporarily. Shortly thereafter, the oil and vinegar will separate once again. A permanent emulsion requires the use of an emulsifier, such as egg yolk. The egg yolk particles will coat both the oil and vinegar particles and keep them suspended in each other rather than separating. To create this, the oil must be whisked in vigorously while adding it very slowly to the other ingredients. All emulsifications, whether temporary or permanent, always work better at room temperature, as oil is harder to breakdown when it is cold.

Mayonnaise is basically an emulsion of egg and oil. Dressings made with mayonnaise as a base are very popular as well. Potato salad is a classic example of this. Mayonnaise however, is in drastic need of additional flavours in order for it to become a great salad dressing. Please don't be afraid to experiment, as some of the best dressings come from being creative and trying something new. Most importantly, it is a necessity to taste and re-season once the salad has been assembled with the dressing. Potatoes or pasta, for example, on their own are very bland. They will definitely reduce the impact of flavour in the dressing. Have you ever been to a picnic when someone has volunteered to bring the potato salad, and it tasted incredibly bland? You automatically think to yourself "did they even taste this?"

Salad dressings can also be made from other ingredient bases such as sour cream or yogurt. While these would be replacements for a mayonnaise based dressing, they do lack the richness mayonnaise provides. However, low or non-fat varieties of sour cream or yogurt would be ideal for accommodating a lower fat diet. Please keep in mind that these may be low in fat and high in protein, but they are also high in carbohydrates. Therefore they would not suit all forms of dieting.

As previously mentioned, the main focus, on whatever dressing one is making, should be on developing flavour.

> Dear Chef Dez:
> I always have trouble making Caesar Salad dressing. I always make sure I add the oil very slowly when combining, however it always separates rather than coming together to form a nice creamy dressing. I know the egg I'm using in the recipe is supposed to keep it together. What am I doing wrong?
>
> Leah L.
> Abbotsford, BC
>
>
> Dear Leah:
> Three things come to mind immediately. One is, as I mentioned above, to make sure that the ingredients (especially the oil) are as close to room temperature as possible. Two, if the recipe calls for the use of whole eggs, substitute for just egg yolks, as they

are the emulsifying ingredients, not the egg whites. For example, use two egg yolks to replace one whole egg. Three, add the oil in a slow stream into the other ingredients using a food processor, rather than hand whisking. If your dressing still "breaks", all is not lost. Take the broken dressing out of the processor, and puree another egg yolk while adding the broken dressing in a slow steady stream. The extra egg yolk should help to emulsify it properly.

Caesar Salad Dressing

"Do not substitute whole egg for the egg yolks – egg yolks are an emulsifier that will keep this dressing from separating"

1 tbsp lemon juice
1 tbsp white wine vinegar
1 tbsp Dijon mustard
1 tsp Worcestershire sauce
2 dashes tobasco sauce
2 ½ (two and one half) anchovies
3 crushed garlic cloves
2 egg yolks
2 tbsp dry dill
½ (one half) tsp salt
1 cup canola oil

1. Process all of the ingredients, except for the canola oil, in a food processor.
2. With the food processor running at top speed, gradually and the oil in a very slow steady stream until fully incorporated.

Makes approximately 2 cups

Bocconcini Salad with Balsamic Reduction

Full colour photo available at www.chefdez.com

"An Italian classic, but simple recipe that celebrates the tastes of fresh basil with tomatoes and baby mozzarella"

BALSAMIC REDUCTION DRESSING

1 cup balsamic vinegar
¼ (one quarter) cup dark brown sugar

SALAD

4 Roma tomatoes, sliced thin
8 to 9 balls of bocconcini cheese, sliced thin
Fresh basil leaves

1 Bring the balsamic vinegar to a boil over medium-high heat. Reduce the heat to medium-low and simmer until the volume of the vinegar has reduced to approximately ¾ (three quarters) of a cup. *Make sure you have your overhead fan on high, and be careful to not breath in the strong vinegar fumes directly.
2 Stir in the brown sugar until completely dissolved. Remove from heat and refrigerate until cool.
3 While the dressing is cooling, arrange the tomatoes, cheese, and basil leaves in an alternating circular display on four plates.
4 Drizzle the cooled balsamic reduction over the salads and serve immediately.

Makes 4 portions

Fat Free Coleslaw Dressing

"Creamy and flavourful – no one will ever guess that it is fat free"

1 cup no-fat yogurt
1 cup no-fat sour cream
¼ (one quarter) cup powdered buttermilk

¼ (one quarter) cup liquid honey

1 tbsp yellow mustard

1 tbsp apple cider vinegar

1 tbsp finely grated red onion

1 tsp Worcestershire sauce

1 tsp salt

½ (one half) tsp seasoning salt

½ (one half) tsp freshly ground pepper

½ (one half) tsp sambal oelek, optional

1 Place all ingredients in a mixing bowl. Whisk thoroughly to combine.
2 Keep refrigerated until needed. Toss with your favorite coleslaw ingredients, like green cabbage, purple cabbage, grated carrots, etc.

Makes approximately 2 ½ (two and one half) cups

Mediterranean Salad Dressing

"Dress your salad immediately after mixing, as this dressing will separate if left standing"

½ (one half) cup extra-virgin olive oil

¼ (one quarter) cup balsamic vinegar

¼ (one quarter) cup lemon juice

¼ (one quarter) cup oil packed sundried tomatoes, drained & finely chopped

1 large garlic clove, crushed

2 tbsp liquid honey

½ (one half) tsp salt

½ (one half) tsp fresh cracked pepper

1 Place all ingredients in a bowl, and whisk thoroughly to combine. Pour immediately over your choice of greens.
2 Alternatively, place all ingredients in a glass jar with a lid, and shake thoroughly before serving.

Makes approximately 1 ¼ (one and one quarter) cups

Greek Salad

Full colour photo available at www.chefdez.com

"The longer the dressing stays on the salad, the more juices will come out of the vegetables. If you like it very crisp, serve within a couple hours – if you like the vegetables softer, then let it sit overnight. Either way, be sure to re-season before serving."

2 long English cucumbers, diced ¾ (three quarter) inch
4 medium tomatoes, or 6-8 roma tomatoes, diced ¾ (three quarter) inch
1 large yellow pepper, diced ¾ (three quarter) inch
1 large orange pepper, diced ¾ (three quarter) inch
1 medium to large red onion, diced ¾ (three quarter) inch
1 cup whole kalamata olives

DRESSING

1 cup olive oil
1/4 (one quarter) cup fresh lemon juice
3 tbsp red wine vinegar
2 tbsp dried oregano leaves
2 garlic cloves, crushed
1 tbsp sugar
Salt and coarsely ground pepper to season
Crumbled feta cheese to garnish

1 In a large bowl, toss the vegetables and olives together.
2 In a separate bowl, mix the dressing ingredients well and pour over the salad. Toss to coat.
3 Store in refrigerator for at least 2 hours or overnight, stirring occasionally.
4 Scoop into salad bowl with a slotted spoon, and toss back in the desired amount of the dressing leftover.
5 Garnish with crumbled feta cheese.

Makes 4 to 8 servings.

Quick & Easy
Oil & Vinegar Salad Dressing

½ (one half) cup extra virgin olive oil

¼ - 1/3 (one quarter to one third) cup balsamic vinegar

1 tbsp liquid honey

½ (one half) tsp dried basil leaves

½ (one half) tsp dried oregano leaves

½ (one half) tsp salt

¼ (one quarter) tsp fresh cracked pepper

1 garlic clove, crushed

1 Put all ingredients in a jar with a lid.

2 Shake to combine and pour immediately over salad greens of your choice.

Makes approximately ¾ (three quarter) cup

9

Creating Flavour when Cooking Meat

For many of us, meat is an important part of our daily diet. Whether it be beef, lamb, pork or chicken, it is important to know the basics of creating the most flavour possible.

Marinades seem to be first and foremost in people's minds when it comes to creating flavour in cooked meats. Although they do create flavour, they are also important in making a cut of meat more tender. The best marinades are made up from the simplest of ingredients that you have in your home already. Please don't rely on the packages of powder you find at the supermarkets. Marinades are made up from a base, an acid, and flavourful ingredients. The base of a marinade is usually oil, as this will aid in the cooking process. An acid such as vinegar, wine, or lemon juice is added to breakdown the tougher proteins found in the meat. Red meats and pork, depending on the cuts, are the toughest and are better to marinate from one hour up to twenty-four hours. Chicken proteins are much more delicate and are more preferably marinated for no longer than four hours. Over marinated chicken will actually start to become tough. The same follows through with seafood, as it's protein composition is even more fragile than chicken. Seafood should usually be marinated for a mere 30 minutes to an hour.

The flavour combinations that can be added to a marinade are literally endless.

Crushed garlic, herbs, spices, and condiments, are just a few. Be creative!

Flavour creation does not only exist by marinating. Searing meats, marinated or not, is very important. There is virtually no cooking method that should exempt one from searing meat first. This develops a crust that will carry flavour all the way through to the finished dish one is preparing. Stew, for example, has a more developed beef flavour when the stew meat pieces are browned prior to the addition of other ingredients.

Many presume searing seals juices inside the meat. This, however, is incorrect as no amount of searing can prevent the loss of moisture.

The flavour in crust development can be enhanced even further by the addition of seasoning. If the meat has not been marinating, you may want to add salt & pepper to the meat prior to searing. This simple seasoning will then become part of the meat's outer shell. Applying dry rubs, consisting of a mixture of many different spices, prior to searing is popular for adding a complexity of flavours.

Searing should be done at a high temperature with an amount of oil that prevents sticking. Do not crowd the pan or surface area, as this will decrease the temperature and cause the meat to simmer in its juices rather than caramelize. Searing also creates "browned bits" (called fond) on the bottom of a pan. Fond will also add depth in flavour to a sauce being created. To achieve this, add a liquid, such as wine or stock, to the pan and loosen these bits with a wooden spoon. Use this liquid as a part of the sauce, or reduce it further it to become a sauce of its own. The reduction process of this liquid will cause water to evaporate thus concentrating the flavours and creating a desired sauce consistency. Taste and adjust the sauce as necessary prior to serving.

> Dear Chef Dez:
> I heard that it important to let a beef roast "rest" when it comes out of the oven, before carving it. Is this true, and why?
>
> Brad B.
> Abbotsford, BC

> Dear Brad:
> This is true. Actually it is true with all cuts of meat, not just beef roasts. The "resting" period gives the meat time to adjust coming from the extreme heat to room temperature. During the cooking process, the high heat causes the atoms in the molecular structure of the meat to move at a high rate of speed. If the meat is cut into soon after it has been removed from the oven, grill, or pan, it will lose a large degree of its vital juices that keep it moist and flavourful.

Blackening Cajun Spice

"A perfect way to add tons of flavour. Store in an air-tight container for 3 to 6 months."

¼ (one quarter) cup paprika
2 tsp ground dried oregano
2 tsp ground black pepper
2 tsp salt
1 tsp ground dried thyme
½ (one half) tsp cayenne pepper, or more if you like it hotter

1 Mix all ingredients together.
2 Use it to liberally coat meat, poultry, or fish before grilling or pan-frying.
3 Finish cooked product with a drizzle of garlic butter.

Makes approximately ¼ (one quarter) cup

Cinnamon Roasted Pork Tenderloin with Pinot Gris Applesauce

Full colour photo available at www.chefdez.com

"The tenderloin is brined in salt water to help keep it juicy and flavourful"

4 cups cold water
¼ (one quarter) cup table salt
1 pound pork tenderloin
1 tbsp cinnamon
1 tsp paprika
½ (one half) tsp salt
¼ (one quarter) tsp pepper
¼ (one quarter) tsp cumin
1 tbsp olive oil
1 tsp liquid honey
Fresh mint leaves (for garnish), optional

APPLESAUCE

½ (one half) cup Pinot Gris, or other white wine
1 tsp lemon juice
2 large Granny Smith apples, peeled, cored, & sliced thin
1 tbsp white sugar
¼ (one quarter) tsp allspice
Pinch of salt

1 Dissolve the ¼ (one quarter) cup table salt in the 4 cups of water. Add the tenderloin, and brine for one hour in the refrigerator.
2 Remove the tenderloin and pat dry. Mix the next seven ingredients in a small bowl to make a wet rub. Apply this rub to all areas of the tenderloin, and let sit in the refrigerator for ½ (one half) hour to 12 hours.
3 Preheat the oven to 400 degrees. Roast the tenderloin in the oven for 20 to 25 minutes. Let sit for 5 to 10 minutes before slicing. Serve with the applesauce, and garnish with a mint leaf sprig.

APPLESAUCE

1 Add all the ingredients for the applesauce to a non-reactive (stainless steel) pot.
2 Bring to a boil over medium-high heat while breaking up the apples with a wooden spoon.
3 Lower the heat to medium-low and simmer for 20 minutes.
4 Mash the apples until desired consistency is reached, and hold covered off the heat until needed.

Makes 2 - 4 servings

Easy BBQ Pig Sandwich

Full colour photo available at www.chefdez.com

"By using a store bought BBQ sauce, this doesn't get any easier!"

1.5 kg boneless pork rib roast
1 - 425ml bottle Bull's Eye brand BBQ Sauce
1 onion, thinly sliced

6 cloves garlic, chopped

3 tbsp cornstarch

3 tbsp cold water

6 – 8 buns, toasted

6 - 8 thick slices of tomato

6 – 8 lettuce leaves

1 Remove the strings from the roast, if necessary.

2 Place the roast, BBQ sauce, onion, and garlic in a large heavy bottomed pot. Toss to coat and bring to a boil over medium high heat.

3 Place a lid on the pot and reduce the heat to low and simmer for 3 ½ hours, turning the roast over half way through the cooking time.

4 Remove the roast from the pot and place it in a large bowl. Shred the roast into slivers with two forks.

5 Mix the cornstarch and cold water in a small bowl and whisk into the sauce remaining sauce in the large pot. Bring this mixture to a boil to thicken.

6 Pour the thickened BBQ sauce over the shredded pork and mix thoroughly.

7 Serve a mound of the BBQ pork mixture on half of a toasted bun, while topping the other half of the bun with lettuce and tomato.

Makes 6 to 8 servings

Quick Meat Marinade

"The acidity in the red wine tenderizes beef beautifully. Why purchase powdered marinade mixes when you can create something this wonderful with raw ingredients."

¼ (one quarter) cup full bodied red wine

¼ (one quarter) cup olive oil

4 large garlic cloves, pressed

1 tsp salt

1 tsp pepper

1 tsp dried oregano leaves

1 tsp dried basil leaves

½ tsp sambal oelek

1. Mix all ingredients together.
2. Pour over 2 to 4 steaks in a plastic bag. Press out the excess air, seal and let sit refrigerated for one half hour to as much as eight hours. Tougher, less expensive cuts of beef will benefit more from the longer marinating time.
3. Remove steaks from marinade and grill to desired doneness.

Makes enough marinade for 2 to 4 steaks

Garlic & Red Wine Braised Beef with Ham & Gruyère Cheese

Full colour photo available at www.chefdez.com

"Braising transforms tough inexpensive round steaks into a beautifully tender meal"

2 tbsp vegetable oil
6 beef round steaks (individually sized)
Salt and pepper
1 head garlic (12 – 15 cloves), peeled
1 small onion, diced small, approximately ½ (one half) cup
½ (one half) cup full-bodied red wine
1 tbsp flour
1 tbsp butter, room temperature
2 – 3 tsp sugar
300g shaved Black Forest ham
150g grated Gruyère cheese

1. Preheat oven to 300 degrees.
2. Coat the steaks with 1 tbsp of the oil and season them with salt and pepper.
3. Heat a large oven proof pan over medium-high heat. When hot, add the other tbsp of oil to the pan and sear both sides of the steaks until brown – approximately 3 to 4 minutes per side. It is important to not "crowd" the pan as this will inhibit the browning process. If necessary, brown the steaks in 2 batches.
4. Remove the steaks and set aside once browned.
5. Remove the pan from the heat. Deglaze the pan by adding the red wine and

with a wooden spoon scrape the browned bits on the pan into the red wine. This will add a tremendous amount of flavour to the finished sauce. Add the onion and whole garlic cloves to the pan and stir to coat with the wine.

6 Place the steaks in the pan, on top of the garlic cloves and diced onion. Pour any residual liquid from the resting steaks into the pan as well. Cover and bake for 2 hours in the preheated oven.

7 Mix the flour and room temperature butter together in a small bowl and set aside.

8 Once the 2 hour cooking time has completed, remove the steaks and place them on a baking sheet or broiler pan. Top the steaks with equal amounts of the shaved ham and grated cheese. Place the pan under the broiler until the cheese has melted, approximately 2 to 4 minutes.

9 In the meantime, finish the sauce by straining the pan liquids through a wire mesh strainer and push the solids through the strainer with a wooden spoon into the strained liquids. This will eliminate any solids of onion or garlic and make it easier to incorporate these flavours into the sauce.

10 Return this strained sauce back to the pan and over medium-high heat whisk in small parts of the butter/flour mixture until the desired thickness is reached – it should just coat the back of a spoon. Remember the sauce must reach the boiling point in order to achieve the full thickening power of the flour and to remove the starchy taste of the flour. Season the sauce to taste with the sugar, salt and pepper. Once the sauce is done, remove it from the heat and cover it to stop any evaporation.

11 Plate the steaks and drizzle with equal amounts of the sauce.

Makes 6 portions

Grandma G's BBQ Ribs

"When my Mom was a child, they raised pigs on a farm, and my Grandma would make ribs quite often with a homemade BBQ sauce very similar to this."

2 or 3 racks of pork baby-back ribs
Salt & Pepper for seasoning
½ (one half) cup ketchup

¼ (one quarter) cup HP Sauce

¼ (one quarter) cup brown sugar

2 tbsp white vinegar

1 tbsp lemon juice

½ (one half) tsp pepper

½ (one half) tsp salt

½ (one half) tsp cinnamon

Dash of cloves

2 garlic cloves, crushed

2 tsp vegetable oil (however, if you want to keep this recipe closer to the original used by my Grandma, use 2 tsp melted butter as they didn't have vegetable oil on the farm)

1. Preheat the oven to 450 degrees.
2. Season both sides of the ribs with salt and pepper and place them on a cookie sheet(s).
3. Sear the ribs in the oven for 30 minutes. While ribs are searing, mix all the remaining ingredients to create the BBQ sauce.
4. Remove the ribs from the oven and lower the oven temperature to 300 degrees.
5. Brush the ribs on both sides with the BBQ sauce. Pour ½ (One half) cup water onto the cookie sheet and put the ribs back onto the cookie sheet. Cover the sheet with enough aluminum foil to tightly seal over the edges of the cookie sheet (this will hold in the steam that will slowly cook the ribs).
6. Place inside the oven and bake at 300 degrees for 1-½ (one and one half) hours.
7. Lower the oven temperature to 250 degrees and bake for another 1-½ (one and one half) hours. It is very important to not open up the sealed tray of ribs.
8. Remove the tray of ribs and turn the oven to "broil".
9. ALL OF THE FOLLOWING STEPS MUST BE DONE CAREFULLY, AS THE RIBS ARE NOW SO TENDER THAT THE MEAT WILL FALL OFF THE BONES.
10. Pierce the aluminum foil in the corner and gently pour out the water.
11. Remove and discard the aluminum foil. Gently brush the top of the ribs liberally with the sauce.
12. Broil the ribs on the tray in the oven for a few minutes until the sauce on the top has caramelized.
13. Gently remove the ribs off the tray and transfer onto a serving platter by sliding a couple of long utensils (tongs, for example) underneath each rack in order to not disturb the shape of the racks.

Makes 4 to 6 servings

Greek Souvlaki

Full colour photo available at www.chefdez.com

"This recipe is best with metal skewers – if using wooden skewers, soak them in water to help prevent burning."

"Chicken breast proteins are more fragile than red meat proteins, thus requires less marinating time – over marinated chicken will become tough."

1.5 to 2 pounds leg of lamb, approximately 1 inch cubes
OR
1.5 to 2 pounds beef stew meat, approximately 1 inch cubes
OR
1.5 to 2 pounds chicken breast filets
2/3 (two thirds) cup olive oil
1/3 (one third) cup fresh lemon juice
1 tbsp white wine vinegar
3 garlic cloves, crushed
1 tbsp dried oregano leaves (not ground)
2 to 3 dried bay leaves, crumbled
Salt and pepper to season

1. Place lamb, beef or chicken in a large zip-lock bag.
2. Mix all other ingredients in a bowl, and pour into bag of lamb, beef or chicken.
3. Seal the bag leaving as little air as possible; toss around to coat.
4. Let marinate in fridge (24 hours for lamb/beef or 3 to 4 hours for chicken), tossing around occasionally.
5. If using wooden skewers, soak them in cold water for at least 2 hours to help prevent them from burning. For metal skewers, spray with non-stick spray.
6. Put meat on skewers; the number of skewers you will need, will depend of the number of pieces you want to serve per portion. Be thorough in removing all of the bits of bay leaves from the meat as they can be a choking hazard.
7. Grill skewers over a medium to medium-high heat turning occasionally until done, approximately 10-20 minutes depending on the temperature of your grill.
8. Serve warm, still on skewers, on a bed of rice, and tzatziki for dipping (see recipe in Chapter 1).

Makes 4 to 6 servings.

Mediterranean Stuffed Pork Loin Roast

Full colour photo available at www.chefdez.com

"I have received more compliments on this recipe than any other"

400g Italian sausage
½ (one half) cup chopped & drained sundried tomatoes (packed in oil)
1/3 (one third) cup grated Parmesan cheese
6 garlic cloves, crushed
1 egg
2 tsp fennel seeds
1 tsp dried oregano leaves
1 tsp freshly ground pepper
½ (one half) tsp dried basil leaves
¼ (one quarter) tsp salt
1 kg boneless pork loin roast
1/3 (one third) cup finely crumbled feta cheese
Fresh spinach leaves
Cotton butcher's twine
Salt & pepper
2 tbsp vegetable/canola oil

1. Preheat oven to 350 degrees.
2. Squeeze sausage from casings into a medium sized mixing bowl.
3. Add the tomatoes, Parmesan, garlic, egg, fennel, oregano, pepper, basil, and salt to the sausage, and mix together.
4. To flatten the roast for stuffing: With a large knife, cut the bottom 1/3 (one third) of the roast lengthwise without cutting through the opposite side. Continue to cut the remaining 2/3 (two thirds) of the roast in half lengthwise. The result should be one long, thin rectangle of pork.
5. Spread the sausage mixture evenly across the pork, leaving a ½ inch border around the edge.
6. Press the crumbled feta cheese evenly into the sausage mixture.
7. Lay a single layer of spinach leaves over the entire surface of the sausage and cheese.
8. Gently roll up the roast; back in the same direction that it was cut to its original shape, making sure that it is not too tight. Tie the roast firmly with

loops of the butcher's twine every 1 inch all the way across the roast. Finish tying with one more loop lengthwise to fully secure the roast/stuffing.

9 Season the outside of the roast liberally with salt and pepper.

10 Heat a large heavy bottomed pan over medium-high heat. Add the vegetable oil and sear the roast on all sides until completely browned.

11 Place the roast on a rack in a shallow baking pan, insert a meat thermometer, and bake until the internal temperature reaches 170 degrees Fahrenheit, approximately 2 hours.

12 Remove from the oven and let it rest for 15 minutes before carving and serving.

Makes 6 to 8 servings

10

Cranberries and Sweet Potatoes for Thanksgiving

The autumn season is finally here! This is my favorite time of the year. The changing of the leaves, the crispness in the air, and of course the food! Considering that Thanksgiving is fast approaching, I think it would be interesting to discuss some of the essentials included in a classic Thanksgiving dinner. Today, I will be focusing on cranberries and sweet potatoes.

In North America it is very traditional to serve cranberries with our Thanksgiving Day turkey. It is called sauce, but is more like a form of jam or jelly. Cranberries on their own are very acidic and therefore are not eaten raw, and very welcoming to the addition of sugar. These berries are a very durable fruit and thus their fall harvesting method is very unique. After being mechanically removed from their bushes, the fields are then flooded. The cranberries float to the surface before being collected.

Cranberries are available to us in the supermarkets in a variety of forms. Although they are only available to us fresh in autumn, canned prepared jellies and jams still are the most frequently purchased. When buying fresh, as with most fruit, look for ones that are plump, unblemished and bright in colour. They are also available frozen and in juice varieties. Cranberries are a natural astringent and therefore known to be good for blood circulation, complexion, digestion, and in the treatment of urinary-tract infections.

Try making a cranberry sauce from fresh cranberries this year. There are many recipes available and you will find it a very tasty and satisfying change. It is a perfect item to prepare in advance of the holiday weekend.

Sweet potatoes and yams are also another favorite this time of year. Many are confused about the two different varieties. Sweet potatoes have orange coloured flesh, while yams are starchier, less flavourful, and have white flesh. The names are usually mismatched with each other. Sweet potatoes (with orange flesh) are the more popular of the two, and therefore will be our focus.

These potatoes are completely different from the standard potato varieties we find in the supermarkets such as russets and Yukon golds. In fact, sweet potatoes are not botanically potatoes at all. They are a root vegetable plant related to a beautiful flowering vine called Morning Glory, which is commonly planted as an annual and produces trumpet like flowers in an array of colours.

Sweet potatoes are a very healthy alternative to potatoes. Despite the fact that they have just as many carbohydrates they have much higher nutritional value. They are loaded with beta carotene (recognizable from their orange colour) and are high in vitamins A and C. They have a moist, sweet texture, are low in sodium, and make an excellent source of fiber when eaten with the skin. They are very versatile and can be prepared in just as many ways as standard potatoes. They are even excellent in some desserts due to their natural sweetness. Try something new with sweet potatoes this Thanksgiving – your body will thank you!

Dear Chef Dez:
I like the taste of sweet potatoes, but all I ever do is either bake them or boil/mash them. What do you recommend for something different to try?

Beverly H.
Mission, BC

Dear Beverly:
One of my favorite accompaniments for a turkey dinner is a sweet potato soup starter. It is basically a puree that is thinned out further with milk/cream to make a soup. I flavour it with salt, white pepper, cloves, nutmeg, and of course a bit of garlic! Other things you can do are endless: candied yams, Sheppard's pie, grilled slices, pasta, stir-fry's, and in any application that you would normally use regular potatoes. Try serving them with sour cream or mixing a little in for a different flavour. The Internet and the library are great resources to discover new and exciting recipes. Most of all have fun!

Brandied Cranberry Sauce

"Very intense flavour – a homemade cranberry sauce to be proud of"

1 – 340g package fresh cranberries (approximately three and one half cups)
½ (one half) cup packed dark brown sugar
½ (one half) cup brandy
2 cinnamon sticks, broken in half
Zest of 1 lemon, finely chopped
Pinch of salt

1. Combine all ingredients in a heavy bottomed medium-sized pot. Turn heat to medium-high and bring to a boil uncovered.
2. Once boiling, reduce the heat to medium and continue to cook mixture for approximately 10 to 15 minutes until desired consistency is reached, while occasionally stirring and mashing berries with a wooden spoon.
3. Remove from the heat; transfer the sauce into a different container and cool in the refrigerator. Once cooled, remove the cinnamon sticks and serve.

Makes approximately 2 cups

Cranberry Almond Coffee Cake

Full colour photo available at www.chefdez.com

"This rich, intensely flavoured cake is perfect with a cup of coffee, and the cranberries make it extraordinary"

2/3 (two thirds) cup packed dark brown sugar
1/3 (one third) cup butter
1 ½ (one and one half) cup cranberries
½ (one half) cup sliced almonds
½ (one half) cup butter, room temperature
½ (one half) cup white sugar
¼ (one quarter) cup dark brown sugar
2 eggs

1 tbsp instant coffee

1 tsp vanilla

1 cup sour cream

¼ (one quarter) cup milk

1 ½ (one and one half) cups flour

1 ½ (one and one half) tsp baking powder

1 tsp baking soda

½ (one half) tsp cinnamon

1/8 (one eighth) tsp cloves

1/8 (one eighth) tsp nutmeg

¼ (one quarter) tsp salt

1 Preheat oven to 350 degrees. Line a 9-inch spring-form pan with aluminum foil to prevent leaking, and spray the entire inside of the pan with baking spray.

2 In a small pot, combine the 2/3 (two thirds) cup brown sugar and the 1/3 (one third) cup butter. Bring to a boil over medium heat. Pour into the spring-form pan and sprinkle evenly with cranberries and sliced almonds.

3 In a large mixing bowl, cream the butter together with both sugars until light and fluffy. Beat the eggs in one at a time. Stir in the instant coffee and vanilla.

4 Combine the sour cream and milk together and set aside.

5 Combine all of the remaining dry ingredients and set aside.

6 Beat in the flour mixture alternatively with the sour cream mixture, until all three parts become one batter.

7 Pour the batter into the spring-form pan over the cranberries and almonds.

8 Bake for 1 hour or until an inserted toothpick comes out clean.

9 Cool in pan for 10 minutes before inverting onto a serving plate. Carefully remove the pan and serve while still warm.

Makes one 9-inch cake.

Cranberry Pistachio Banana Bread

Full colour photo available at www.chefdez.com

"The half slice of banana on the top of the loaf gives this loaf a unique recognizable presentation"

½ (one half) cup butter, room temperature

1 cup sugar

½ (one half) cup dark brown sugar

4 eggs

2 cups mashed very ripe bananas (approximately 4 to 6)

3 cups flour

4 tsp baking powder

1 tsp baking soda

1 tsp cinnamon

½ (one half) tsp salt

2 cups cranberries, roughly chopped, thawed if frozen

1 ½ (one and one half) cups shelled salted pistachio nuts, left whole

1 yellow banana, sliced in half lengthwise

1. Preheat the oven to 350 degrees and prepare two loaf pans by spraying with baking spray.

2. Beat the butter and both sugars together with an electric mixer until thoroughly combined, approximately 2 minutes. Turn the speed to med-low and add 1 egg at a time until all 4 eggs are completely blended in. Stir in the mashed bananas.

3. In a large separate bowl add the flour, baking powder, baking soda, cinnamon, salt, and stir to combine. Add the cranberries and pistachios to this dry mixture to coat them with flour.

4. Add the wet egg/sugar/banana mixture to the dry ingredients and fold together until just combined – do not overmix.

5. Divide the batter between the two loaf pans and smooth out until even.

6. Place ½ of the yellow banana (cut side down) on the batter in each of the pans and bake for approximately 55 to 65 minutes, or until a toothpick inserted comes out clean.

Makes 2 loaves

Sweet Potato Pesto Gratin

"A rich and decadent vegetable side dish"

1 kg sweet potato
Salt & pepper
Baking spray
1 recipe parsley pesto (from Chapter 3)
¼ (one quarter) cup Parmesan cheese

1 Peel and cut the sweet potato into ½ (one half) inch cubes.
2 Steam the potato cubes for approximately 20 minutes until fork tender.
3 Preheat the oven to 400 degrees.
4 Prepare the recipe of parsley pesto.
5 In a mixing bowl, mash the cooked sweet potato into a smooth consistency. Season to taste with salt & pepper.
6 Spray a 9 x 9 inch, or a 9 x 11 inch pan with baking spray.
7 Spread ½ (one half) of the potato mixture evenly in the pan.
8 Spread ½ (one half) of the pesto evenly over the squash.
9 Repeat with the remaining potato mixture and then pesto.
10 Sprinkle Parmesan cheese over the surface evenly and bake for 15 minutes. Turn the oven to broil and continue cooking until the top has browned.
11 Remove from the oven and let stand for at least 10 minutes before serving.

Makes 4 to 6 portions

Sweet Potato Spinach Patties with Pomegranate Demi-Glaze

Full colour photo available at www.chefdez.com

"An easy, nutritional, gourmet dish to serve with leftover turkey"

1 pound orange sweet potato, peeled, diced ½ (one half) inch
1 pkg frozen chopped spinach thawed and drained
100g feta cheese, finely crumbled

2 eggs
2/3 (two thirds) cup cornflake crumbs
2 garlic cloves, finely chopped
1 tsp salt
½ (one half) tsp ground black pepper
Olive oil

1. Steam the sweet potato for 15 to 20 minutes until tender. Let cool to room temperature in a large bowl.
2. Add the spinach, feta, eggs, corn flake crumbs, garlic, salt, and pepper to the sweet potato and mix thoroughly.
3. Divide into 6 equal amounts and press into round ¾ (three quarter) inch thick patties.
4. Heat a nonstick frying pan to medium heat. Drizzle pan with minimal amount of olive oil. Fry patties for approximately 6 or 7 minutes per side until browned.

Seeds from 2 pomegranates
¼ (one quarter) cup water
4 garlic cloves, roughly chopped
2 tsp concentrated chicken stock paste
¼ (one quarter) tsp ground cloves
¼ (one quarter) tsp cracked black pepper
1 tbsp cold water
1 tsp cornstarch

1. Place the seeds, water, garlic cloves, chicken stock paste, cloves, and pepper in a small saucepan over medium heat. Bring to a boil and simmer for approximately ten minutes.
2. Remove from heat, cover and let stand for ten minutes.
3. Strain through a wire mesh strainer into a bowl. You should end up with approximately one half cup of juice. Place this juice back into the saucepan and discard the seeds.
4. Whisk cornstarch into the water and then whisk into the pomegranate juice. Bring to a boil over medium high heat to thicken. Cover and remove from heat until ready to serve.
5. Place one patty on the center of each plate. Top with left over sliced turkey and drizzle with the pomegranate demi-glaze.

Makes 6 portions

11

Seasonal Beverages for the Winter Months

The upcoming holiday season is a very special time of the year that is celebrated not only with food, but with favorite drinks as well. Family and friends come together to eat, drink, and commemorate the precious relationships that they hold with each other. Throughout the years there have been many beverages made to help capture the essence of the season and these gatherings.

Eggnog is probably the first seasonal beverage that comes to mind. Eggnog is a drink that seems to have originated in Britain from a drink called a posset. This was a mixture of eggs, milk, and ale, sherry, or brandy. Posset was served in small, carved, wooden mugs called "noggins", and thus the name "eggnog" was created. In North America the recipe was altered with rum as the replacement for the ale, sherry, or brandy.

In today's world, eggnog is not necessarily served with alcohol and is a favorite for many of all ages. There are numerous recipes available to make eggnog from scratch, but most just buy it pre-made in a carton. The varieties available to us at our local grocery stores also include a light version that is lower in fat, and at some locations, a no-fat variety. It is mostly served chilled either with or without ice, but I prefer to served it hot, individually, like a steamed milk, and garnished with a sprinkle of freshly grated nutmeg. If you aren't likely to make your eggnog from a recipe, at least buy whole nutmeg versus pre-ground, and try it grating it fresh onto the eggnog before serving. The flavour difference is incredible.

Hot apple cider and mulled wines are other wintertime favorites. These creations are made by heating either cider or red wine with a combination of favorite spices to infuse flavour. There is an endless combination of spices that one can use, such as cinnamon, nutmeg, cloves, star anise, and many other warm complimenting flavours. Sugar is not usually added to hot apple ciders as the base cider used in the recipe already provides an abundance of natural sweetness from the apples. Mulled wines require a bit of sugar to compliment the feeling of consuming a warm festive drink, while also offsetting some of the acidity in the wine. Mulled wines that are heated for a long period of time are less likely to contain as much residual alcohol. Many prefer to have most of the alcohol still left in the finished product and thus cook it briefly. Whichever way you choose to serve and consume this wonderful seasonal favourite, just remember not to boil the wine. Boiling the wine will rapidly increase the amount of evaporation and risk the chance of the mulled wine being too strong tasting in the end.

A Swedish and Finnish version of mulled wine is called glogg. It is much sweeter and always has a high alcohol content. The final touch to glogg is the addition of a few almonds and raisins to each glass being served. Mulled wines are documented to have been in existence from as early as 400 A.D. in European areas, and thus have quite the history.

Always remember that seasonal beverages do not have to contain alcohol to be enjoyable. A heated cranberry juice, for example, with the same warming spices can be made to replace mulled wine. Furthermore, there are so many choices of fantastic herbal teas and syrups for coffees that capture the essence of the season beautifully. Whatever beverage you choose to help celebrate during the holidays, please drink responsibly.

> Dear Chef Dez:
> I have a recipe for mulled wine that says it should be simmered. Isn't simmering actually a slow boil? I heard you weren't supposed to boil mulled wine – is this correct?
> Erik W.
> Abbotsford, BC

> Dear Erik:
> The culinary definition of simmering is "to cook in water or other liquid that is bubbling gently." Although, this is not the same as a "slow boil," I still would not have my mulled wine heated to this degree. Instead, I prefer just to warm it thoroughly for approximately 30 to 45 minutes to the maximum point of having wisps of steam rising from the surface.

Homemade Eggnog

"The constant stirring of the egg mixture, while it is cooking, is vital to ensure that the eggs don't become scrambled eggs"

6 egg yolks
½ (one half) cup sugar
1 cup whipping cream
1 cup whole milk
½ (one half) tsp ground nutmeg
Pinch of salt
1 additional cup of whipping cream
6 tbsp dark or spiced rum

1. In a stainless steel bowl, whisk the egg yolks with the sugar until smooth.
2. Mix in the 1 cup of whipping cream, the milk, nutmeg, and salt until completely combined.
3. Place the bowl over a pot of simmering water. For a more temperate heat, make sure that the water does not touch the bottom of the bowl. Whisk the mixture constantly until it reaches a temperature of 175 degrees Fahrenheit.
4. Remove the bowl from the heat and immediately chill uncovered in the refrigerator until cold.
5. While the mixture is cooling, whisk the remaining cup of whipping cream until soft peaks form.
6. Once the egg mixture is cold, gradually fold it into the whipped cream from the previous step.
7. Stir in the rum, pour into glasses and garnish with more freshly grated nutmeg.

Makes just over 5 cups

Homemade Irish Cream Liqueur

"One may want to purchase pasteurized eggs in a carton if they are not comfortable consuming raw eggs"

1 ½ (one and one half) cups of whiskey
11 oz. can of sweetened condensed milk

1 cup light cream
2 large eggs
1 tsp instant coffee
1 tsp powdered chocolate drink mix
1 tsp vanilla extract
Pinch of salt

1 Blend all ingredients together in a food processor or blender until completely smooth.
2 Dispense into sanitized bottles/lids and refrigerate immediately, and consume within two weeks.

Makes approximately 4 cups.

Hot Apple Cider

"This is so easy – never buy those powdered spiced apple drinks again. For a non-alcoholic version, replace the brandy with a clear juice or nonalcoholic wine."

4 cups apple juice
4 cinnamon sticks
20 whole cloves
15 whole allspice
½ (one half) cup brandy

1 Add all of the ingredients, except for the brandy, to a medium size pot. Bring to a boil over medium heat.
2 Lower heat to medium-low and simmer uncovered until it has reduced to 3 ½ (three and one half) cups in volume, approximately 20 to 30 minutes.
3 Remove from the heat and strain to remove the cinnamon sticks, cloves, and allspice.
4 Stir in the brandy and serve garnished with a cinnamon stick in each mug.

Makes 4 – 1-cup portions

Italian Polenta Buns with Grappa

Full colour photo available at www.chefdez.com

"A favorite in Italy - Freshly baked sweet biscuits reminiscent of rich polenta. Grappa is an Italian Liqueur made from grape remnants after pressing them for wine."

4 tbsp raisins
2 tbsp Italian Grappa liqueur (plus more for sipping)
1 cup fine cornmeal
1 cup milk, heated to almost boiling
1 cup corn flour
2/3 (two thirds) cup sugar
¼ (one quarter) cup all-purpose flour
1 tbsp baking powder
½ (one half) tsp salt
½ (one half) cup cold butter, cut into small pieces
Cold milk, optional
Icing sugar

1 In a small bowl, soak the raisins in the Grappa.
2 Preheat the oven to 425 degrees and prepare a large baking sheet with parchment paper.
3 In a separate bowl, stir the hot milk and the cornmeal together. It will get very thick as the cornmeal swells and absorbs the milk.
4 In another bowl combine all of the other dry ingredients together: corn flour, sugar, all-purpose flour, baking powder, and salt.
5 Work the cold butter pieces into this dry mixture with a pastry cutter until the butter pieces are about the size of peas. Do not work the butter in with your hands, as this will melt the butter.
6 Stir the raisins and Grappa mixture into the milk/cornmeal mixture. Then mix this with the dry ingredients and butter mixture until it is just combined – do not over mix. If it is too dry, add a little extra milk. It should resemble a thick muffin batter.
7 Spoon 8 equal portions onto the prepared baking sheet and bake immediately for 15 minutes or until golden brown.
8 Carefully remove the biscuits from the pan and let cool slightly on a cooling rack. Dust with icing sugar and serve warm with a small shot of Grappa, coffee, or espresso.

Makes 8 biscuits

Mulled Wine

"Red wine Lovers rejoice! This recipe is not overly sweet and will keep you warm inside."

1 - 750ml bottle Merlot, or other full bodied red wine
2 cinnamon sticks
5 whole cloves
10 whole allspice
1 whole nutmeg
¼ (one quarter) cup white sugar
Zest from a large orange
2 tbsp orange brandy

1. Put all ingredients in a pot, except for the brandy.
2. Bring to a simmer, but do not let it boil.
3. Let simmer partially covered for 30 to 45 minutes.
4. Remove from the heat and add the brandy.
5. Pour through a wire mesh strainer, and discard the spices and zest.
6. Serve in small mugs and garnish each with a cinnamon stick (optional).
7. Mulled wine is best served warm, not hot. This allows you to taste the full flavour.

Makes 4 to 6 servings

12

Pies for Holiday Desserts

The fondest memory I have from my childhood is one that I hold dear to my heart. Fitted with an over-sized apron and a smile from ear to ear, I was six years old on a stool rolling out pie pastry along side my Mom. While she made the large pies for the family, I rolled out pastry for miniature imitations formed to the confines of empty, metal chip-dip containers. I was very proud and happy to be a part of the preparation for such a wonderful treat.

Pies are a very traditional way to end a meal on certain holidays throughout the year, and especially at Christmas time. Pumpkin is always a favorite pie among many for the holidays, but numerous different pies can and will be made and enjoyed.

Pies are basically made up of a shell or crust, with a flavourful filling, and can be divided into two groups: baked or unbaked. Baked pies are obviously ones with raw pie shells that are filled and then baked. The unbaked category represents prebaked pie shells that are filled with a prepared filling and then chilled to set before serving. The pie dough that makes up these shells can also be divided into two categories: flaky dough or mealy dough. Flaky dough is usually a pastry that has a mixture of shortening and butter that is "cut in" so that there are small chunks still left in the finished product. This aids in creating steam, which helps with the leavening process and thus creating the flaky texture. Mealy dough is one that is usually made with butter that is mixed in more thoroughly, and when baked has a texture much like tender shortbread. This is because the flour particles are more coated with fat and thus less gluten is formed.

Once you have decided on the type of crust to make, it is time to decide on the filling. Basically there are four choices: fruit, custard, cream, or chiffon. All fillings require the existence of a starch or stabilizer to ensure that it holds together when sliced. Fruit and cream fillings use starches, such as cornstarch for their stability, while custard filling use the stabilization of eggs coagulation for their firmness. Examples of custard pies are ones such as pumpkin, pecan, and key lime pies. Chiffon pies usually use a combination of starch or gelatin with whipped eggs whites folded in.

Baking is a science and recipes are the formulas. For the reasons listed here and for many others, it is important to follow these recipes exactly in order to have a successful outcome. Whatever pie or other dessert you choose to have with your holiday meal, I wish you, your families, friends, and loved ones all the best in health and happiness this holiday season.

Dear Chef Dez:
I have heard and known that it is best to keep pie pastry as cold possible to prevent melting the butter and shortening pieces. What is the best way of doing this?
Douglas C.
Langley, BC

Dear Douglas:
The best way of doing this is to first focus on your ingredients. Make sure you are using ice water instead of cold water, and frozen butter grated into the flour mixture is ideal. The frozen butter particles then are already the required size from the grater and will not suffer from the warm friction of too much mixing or "cutting" it in. Secondly, try not to touch the dough with your hands, as the warmth from them will melt the butter. It is best to form the dough by folding it over consistently with a chilled metal dough cutter. Once the dough is formed, wrap and place it in the refrigerator until thoroughly chilled. Remove and proceed with rolling, ideally on a chilled marble surface. Once shaped, refrigerate for approximately ten more minutes before baking.

Cheddar Apple Turnovers

Full colour photo available at www.chefdez.com

Recipe created by Katherine (Mrs. Chef Dez)
"Pocket pastry that combines the incredible tastes of apples and cheddar"

PASTRY

2 2/3 (two and two thirds) cups flour
2 cups grated old cheddar
1 cup butter, cold
6 to 8 tbsp ice cold water

> 1 Mix grated cheese into flour and cut in butter until mixture resembles coarse meal. Add water 1 tbsp at a time, to moisten flour mixture just enough to hold together. Refrigerate at least ½ (one half) hour.

FILLING

4 tart apples (Granny Smith or Galla) peeled, cored and sliced into small pieces
3 tbsp granulated sugar
3 tbsp cornstarch
½ (one half) tsp cinnamon
3 to 4 tsp butter

> 2 Toss the apples, sugar, cornstarch and cinnamon together to coat apples evenly. Set aside the butter for prior to sealing the turnovers (see step # 4).

EGG WASH

1 egg
1 tbsp water

> 3 Whisk together the egg and water thoroughly.
> 4 Roll pastry to 1/8th (one eighth) inch thick. Cut into twelve 6inch rounds. Moisten edges of pastry with egg wash. Distribute the apple filling onto one half of each of the pastry rounds. Dot each with ¼ (one quarter) tsp of butter and fold to close. Pinch edges closed with the tangs of a fork. Brush tops of turnovers with egg wash and transfer to a lightly greased baking sheet. Cut three vent holes into the top of each turnover. Bake at 350 degrees for 30- 35 minutes until golden brown.

Makes 12 turnovers

Creamy Lime Custard Pie

Full colour photo available at www.chefdez.com

Recipe created by Katherine (Mrs. Chef Dez)
"The optional food colouring enhances the presentation of the pie with a bright green lime appeal"

CRUST

¼ (one quarter) Picture Perfect Pie Pastry recipe (this Chapter)

PIE FILLING

1 cup sugar
6 tbsp cornstarch
¼ (one quarter) tsp salt
2 cups milk
3 egg yolks, beaten
¼ (one quarter) cup butter
½ (one half) cup cream cheese, softened in microwave
½ (one half) cup freshly squeezed lime juice
2 tsp finely chopped lime zest
2 to 3 drops green food colouring, optional

MERINGUE TOPPING

3 egg whites
Pinch of cream of tartar
¼ (one quarter) cup icing sugar

1. Roll out the pie crust and line a 9-inch pie plate. Trim the excess off the edge. Flute the edge for presentation. With a fork, poke holes in the bottom and sides of the crust to prevent air bubbles from forming. Blind bake the crust at 450 degrees for 12 to 15 minutes. Let cool at room temperature.
2. In a saucepan, combine the sugar, cornstarch, and salt. Slowly whisk in ¼ (one quarter) cup of the milk. When smooth, whisk in the remainder of the milk. Turn the heat to medium-high and stir constantly until mixture is thick and bubbling. Remove from heat.
3. Slowly whisk 1 cup of the hot milk mixture into the beaten egg yolks, and then pour this yolk mixture back into the hot milk mixture in the saucepan.

Cook and whisk over medium heat for approximately 2 minutes until mixture is very thick and smooth.

4 Remove from the heat and stir in the butter. When the butter is melted, whisk in the softened cream cheese until there are no lumps. Stir in the lime juice, zest, and food colouring. Pour hot filling into baked pie crust.

5 Beat the egg whites and cream of tartar to soft peaks. Gradually add the icing sugar, beating until mixture forms medium/firm peaks. Immediately spread over the pie filling, ensuring to seal the meringue to the edges of the pie crust to prevent shrinkage.

6 Bake the pie at 350 degrees for 12 to 15 minutes or until meringue is golden brown.

7 Cool the pie to room temperature and refrigerate for at least 8 hours before serving.

Garnish with lime zest and twisted lime slices.

Picture Perfect Pie Pastry

Recipe created by Katherine (Mrs. Chef Dez)

"I like to cut in the shortening and grate the butter for the optimum texture and flavour. This is the combination I prefer, but you can feel free to play around with the ratio of butter to shortening as long as you use a total of 2 ¼ cups of fat. Shortening contributes to a lighter pastry and butter makes a more flavourful pastry."

5 cups flour
3 tsp brown sugar
1 tsp salt
1 tsp baking powder
1 pound shortening very cold
¼ (one quarter) cup butter very cold
1 egg
1 tbsp white vinegar
Water

Combine flour, sugar, salt and baking powder. Cut in shortening with a pastry cutter then, using a medium sized grater, grate the butter in and stir to distribute. In a liquid measuring cup, lightly beat egg and vinegar and add enough water to fill to ¾ (three quarters) cup measure. Stir into the flour mixture just until moistened, and divide the dough into four equal portions. Shape each into a flat disk and wrap in plastic wrap. Refrigerate for at least ½ (one half) hour, and then roll out.

This recipe makes enough pastry for two double-crusted pies, and it freezes well.

Pumpkin Chiffon Pie

Recipe created by Katherine (Mrs. Chef Dez)

"Beating the egg whites separately and folding them in makes for a light chiffon texture. A warm spicy twist on a classic family favorite"

¾ (three quarter) cup dark brown sugar, lightly packed
1 ¾ (one and three quarter) cup (398ml) canned pumpkin puree
¼ (one quarter) tsp salt
½ (one half) tsp cinnamon
¼ (one quarter) tsp nutmeg
¼ (one quarter) tsp ginger
¼ (one quarter) tsp cloves
1 ¼ (one and one quarter) cups milk
2 eggs, separated
Unbaked 9-inch pie crust

1. Lower oven rack to one level below center of oven. Preheat oven to 400 degrees.
2. Mix first seven ingredients together in a large bowl.
3. Stir in milk and beaten egg yolks.
4. Beat egg whites to soft peaks and fold into pumpkin mixture.
5. Pour into unbaked pie shell in a standard 9-inch pie plate.
6. Bake for 1 hour, rotating halfway through baking time.

Makes one 9-inch pie

Royal Apples (Apple Dumplings)

Full colour photo available at www.chefdez.com (PICTURED ON FRONT COVER)

Recipe created by Katherine (Mrs. Chef Dez)
"Basically individual apple pies made with whole apples – an apple lover's favourite"

½ (one half) Picture Perfect Pie Pastry recipe (this Chapter)
4 McIntosh Apples
1 lemon
¼ (one quarter) cup chopped pecans
¼ (one quarter) cup dark brown sugar
1tsp cinnamon
4 tsp orange brandy
2 tsp butter
1 egg

1 Roll pastry to 1/8th (one eighth) inch thickness and cut into four 7-inch squares. Reserve dough scraps. Remove zest from the lemon and squeeze juice into a large bowl of cold water. Peel apples and remove cores with a small melon baller being careful to leave the bottom of the apple intact. Immerse apples in lemon water being sure to wet the entire apple.

2 Mix pecans, brown sugar, cinnamon and ¼ (one quarter) tsp of lemon zest (finely chopped). Remove apples from water and pat dry. Fill each apple with pecan mixture and add 1 tsp of brandy and ½ (one half) tsp butter.

3 Mix egg with 1 tbsp of cold water to make an egg wash.

4 Place an apple in the center of each pastry square. Moisten all edges of one pastry square at a time with egg wash. Bring two adjacent corners of the pastry to the top, center of the apple. Pinch together the edges of pastry all the way to the top. Repeat with the remaining sides to form a square bundle around the apple. (See photo on chefdez.com). Be sure to join the pastry firmly leaving no opening at the top of the apples. If desired cut four leaf shapes with the scrap pastry from step #1. Use the back of a knife to draw veins on the leaves. Use egg wash to "glue" leaves onto the top of the pastry bundles. Cut a few small vent holes in discreet places at the top of each apple. Chill for at least ½ (one half) hour.

5 Preheat oven to 425 degrees. Place the apples on a lightly greased baking sheet. Brush with egg wash and place in oven. Immediately turn oven down to 350 degrees. Bake until pastry is golden brown and steam is coming from pastry vents.

Makes four portions

13

Appetizers to help ring in the New Year

Whether it's a formal champagne event, or just a get-together with loved ones, tasty appetizers are a must for any successful New Year's Eve party. In today's market place, there are so many outlets for one to buy appetizers pre-made from the freezer section, but this eliminates all the fun and creativity. Preparing for an evening of guests should be enjoyable and what you prepare should be an expression of your personality. There are numerous options that are not only delicious, but easy as well.

For fancier events, it is nice to have small morsels of food that people can manage with one hand to "pop" into their mouths. This is extremely helpful when a drink is being held in the other hand and there is an abundance of standing and socializing. A perfect example of this would be canapés. Don't let the fancy French name scare you. They are simply pronounced (can ah pays) and are defined as bite-size open-faced sandwiches. Most canapés consist of a base, a spread, and a garnish. Get the bakery to slice your bread lengthwise and toast these sheets of bread in the oven. Then symmetrically place small dollops of spread on every square inch and cut the bread into the squares that are now mapped out. Garnish each one and place them on a platter. An example of a spread and garnish would be horseradish flavoured cream cheese with small pieces of thin beef and a parsley sprig.

Chicken wings are an extremely popular appetizer, and the price of ones that are already "flavoured and cooked" compared to raw ones is drastic. A simple marinade or sauce can be made from ingredients you most likely have in your refrigerator already like barbeque sauce, ketchup, or hot sauce, mixed with a variety of other ingredients. Half the fun is creating something uniquely yours. Nothing is more satisfying than hearing someone say, "Wow, have you tried Katherine's wings? They're incredible!" The other half of the fun is all the money you will save.

A very extraordinary appetizer would be an Italian antipasto platter. This can be easily assembled as a last minute dish with a collection of morsels normally found in an Italian pantry. Make a quick marinade of equal parts of balsamic vinegar and extra virgin olive oil for artichoke hearts, tomatoes, grilled asparagus, roasted peppers, or any other vegetables you prefer. Arrange these marinated veggies on a platter along with sundried tomatoes, melon pieces wrapped in proscuitto, roasted garlic heads, chunks of Parmesan cheese, and slices of baguette, for example. The possibilities are endless, so be creative. If this seems too intimidating to try, I do offer a cooking class in the New Year that focuses on this, along with some more intricate delicacies to make it exceedingly interesting and delicious. Please check out my website under "Chef Dez Services", and then "group culinary cooking classes".

The options to choose from for the appetizers you are going to serve are immeasurable, but hopefully I have given you some ideas. Food is a great social aspect of bringing people together, and even more wonderful when you have made it from scratch. Celebrate cuisine tonight along with the New Year and have a magnificent time.

> Dear Chef Dez:
> I like to make nachos as an appetizer, but they always seem to be lacking something. Do you have any suggestions?
>
> > Sherri D.
> > Abbotsford, BC

> Dear Sherri:
> In order to make something taste great, you have to stay focused on flavour when you are assembling it. Some simple changes will help you with this. The two main ingredients in nachos are tortilla chips and cheese. Make sure that the chips are lightly salted and of high quality, and if using cheddar, choose the extra-old variety for the most flavour. Then add tasty morsels on each layer such as spiced chicken, black olives, diced tomatoes, green onions, and chilies for example. Most importantly season each layer of cheese with chili powder, salt, and fresh cracked pepper to help bring out the flavours of everything. Serve with sour cream, salsa, guacamole and enjoy!

Canapés for All Occasions

Full colour photo available at www.chefdez.com

"Great for cocktail parties – bite sized open-faced sandwiches that allow a drink to be held in the opposite hand. The number of canapés these recipes make are approximate – it will depend on the thickness of the bread, the amount of spread used, and the size of the shapes cut from the bread."

3 loaves of bread, sliced lengthwise, crusts removed, and toasted

BEEF CANAPÉS

250g container of spread-able cream cheese
4 tsp prepared horseradish
4 tsp Dijon mustard
3 tsp Worcestershire sauce
¼ (one quarter) tsp fresh cracked pepper
Shaved beef from the deli
Fresh parsley

> Mix together the cream cheese, horseradish, mustard, Worcestershire, and pepper. Spread this on sheets of toasted bread. Cut into desired bite sized shapes and garnish each one with a small piece of shaved beef and a parsley sprig.

SMOKED SALMON CANAPÉS

250g container of spread-able cream cheese
100g smoked salmon (skinless, boneless)
1 packed tbsp fresh dill
3 tsp lemon juice
¼ (one quarter) tsp fresh cracked pepper
¼ (one quarter) tsp salt
Fresh dill, red onion, and capers, for garnish

> In a food processor, combine the cream cheese, salmon, dill, lemon juice, salt, and pepper until smooth. Spread this on sheets of toasted bread. Cut into desired bite sized shapes and garnish each one with a small sprig of fresh dill, a small piece of red onion, and a caper.

SUN-DRIED TOMATO CANAPÉS

250g container of spread-able cream cheese

¼ (one quarter) cup drained oil packed sun-dried tomatoes

3 tsp balsamic vinegar

½ (one half) tsp anchovy paste

½ (one half) tsp dried basil leaves

¼ (one quarter) tsp chili powder

¼ (one quarter) tsp fresh cracked pepper

1/8 (one eighth) tsp salt

Sun-dried tomatoes & thinly sliced fresh basil, for garnish

In a food processor, combine the cream cheese, tomatoes, vinegar, dried basil, chili powder, anchovy paste, pepper, and salt until smooth. Spread this on sheets of toasted bread. Cut into desired bite sized shapes and garnish each one with a small piece of sun-dried tomato and a small mound of thinly sliced basil.

With the 3 loaves of bread, this will make approximately 180 canapés (60 of each kind)

Honey Garlic Hot Wings

"The best of both worlds – Honey Garlic Wings and Hot Wings all in one." Make sure you serve these with napkins!"

1 cup liquid honey

1 head of garlic (8 to 10 cloves), crushed

3 to 4 tbsp sambal oelek

1 tbsp chili powder

1 tsp cinnamon

Zest from 2 limes, chopped fine

Juice from 2 limes

Dash of ground cloves

Dash of ground nutmeg

Salt & pepper

2 kg chicken wings

1 to 2 tbsp cornstarch

1 Mix all of the ingredients together (except for the wings and the cornstarch) in a bowl. Put the chicken wings in a large freezer bag and pour this mixture

onto the wings. Seal the bag and distribute this marinade around the wings thoroughly. Let sit in the refrigerator for at least 2 to 4 hours.

2 Preheat the oven to 400 degrees.

3 Lay the wings in a single layer on a large baking sheet. Pour the remaining marinade into a pot.

4 Bake the wings for approximately 25 to 30 minutes until cooked through. While the wings are baking, bring the marinade to a boil over medium-high heat and let boil for approximately one minute, stirring constantly.

5 After the wings have baked, drain the excess liquid from the baking sheet into the marinade in the pot, while keeping the wings on the baking sheet.

6 Mix the cornstarch with a few tablespoons of water until completely dissolved. Stir this cornstarch mixture into the hot marinade. Bring this back to a boil, stirring constantly, and it should transform into a thick sauce almost resembling a paste.

7 Distribute this thickened sauce onto the wings evenly. Return the wings to the oven and broil until the sauce has browned slightly, and caramelized onto the wings.

8 Remove from the oven and let cool slightly before serving.

Loaded Nachos

Full colour photo available at www.chefdez.com

"I jokingly call these 'Man Nachos' – as it will be the biggest display of nachos you have seen! Seasoning each layer with salt, pepper, and chili powder helps to make these very flavourful."

1 to 1.5 pounds lean ground beef
1 package taco seasoning
1 bunch green onions, sliced
375ml can sliced black olives, drained
3 medium tomatoes, diced small, drained
2 to 3 jalapenos, sliced into rings
600g old cheddar, grated
1 ½ (one and one half) - 340g bags thick nacho chips
Salt & pepper

Chili powder
Salsa & sour cream, for serving

1. Brown the ground beef with the taco seasoning and set aside.
2. On a 12 x 18 baking sheet make 3 layers with all the ingredients divided equally. Build each layer in the following order:
   Nacho Chips
   Cheese
   Seasoned Beef
   Tomatoes
   Black Olives
   Green Onions
   Jalapenos
   Salt & Pepper
   Chili Powder
   More Cheese
3. The baking sheet will be full and heaped with ingredients. Bake in a pre-heated 350 degree oven for 10 to 15 minutes until cheese has melted and the nachos are completely warmed through.
4. Serve immediately with side dishes of salsa and sour cream.

Serves 4 to 8 people

Spanikopita

Full colour photo available at www.chefdez.com

"Little triangular pastry pockets of spinach & feta cheese. A Greek favourite."

2 tbsp butter
¼ (one quarter) cup minced white onion
2 garlic cloves, chopped
1 – 300g package frozen chopped spinach, thawed
100g feta cheese, crumbled
1 tsp lemon juice
Salt & pepper to taste

10 sheets frozen phyllo pastry, thawed – keep covered with a cool damp towel
Melted butter

1 Melt butter over medium heat in a nonstick pan.
2 Add the onions and garlic and sauté until soft, about 2 minutes.
3 Add the spinach and cook stirring until all the moisture has evaporated.
4 Transfer this mixture to a bowl and let cool.
5 Preheat the oven to 375 degrees.
6 Stir in the Feta cheese, lemon juice, salt & pepper and set aside.
7 On a clean countertop, take one sheet pf pastry, brush it with butter, and place another sheet on top.
8 Cut lengthwise into eight strips.
9 Place a teaspoon of filling on the bottom left corner of each strip. Fold over the right side to meet the left to form a triangle. Continue folding in this manner until you have reached the top.
10 Place on a parchment covered baking sheet. Brush each one with butter.
11 Bake for approximately 15 minutes, until golden brown and serve warm.

Makes 40 pieces

14

Eating Less Fat for your New Year's Resolution

A popular New Year's resolution is eating healthier and/or having less fat in the foods we eat everyday. Every January one will notice an onslaught of extra people at the gym or on local outdoor running tracks. It seems we all want to be healthy, and sometimes all it takes is some small changes and that are applied gradually to our daily eating habits. Here are a few helpful tips to get you motivated.

Choose what you put in your mouth. I know this may sound odd at first, but no one is force-feeding deep-fried fatty foods into your mouth – you are doing that yourself. Frequently all it takes is a conscious effort to make a healthier choice. Train yourself to keep this thought in the forefront of your mind. Little notes to yourself posted in different areas are great motivators.

Try different low fat cooking methods such as grilling, poaching, and non-stick sautéing. Poaching in a savory broth or wine is a great way to not only infuse flavour but also keep your chicken or fish extremely moist. I find that poaching is very misunderstood. It is not the same as "boiling". One of the last things I would want to eat is boiled chicken, for example. The culinary definition of poaching is "to cook gently in water or other liquid that is hot but not actually bubbling, about 160 to 180 degrees Fahrenheit. Wine poached salmon with a dollop of seasoned no-fat sour cream is amazingly delicious.

Most often it is what we add to our food that is fattening rather than the food itself. Try topping your main course with a no-fat salsa. This can be made traditionally with tomatoes, or try the contrasting flavour appeal of a fruit salsa on your steak, chicken, or seafood. If this sounds like too much preparation there are premade jarred varieties available. If salsas don't entice your appetite, then try making different sauces from no-fat yogurt or sour cream. Many recipes are available at the local library or on the internet.

An easy way to reduce your daily intake of fat is by making small changes to the items you consume regularly. Milk is a great example. For argument's sake, let's assume you want to make the switch from homogenized to skim milk, but the change is too drastic. Make the transition by taking small gradual steps to achieve this goal. For the first month make the switch from homogenized to 2% milk until you get used to it. On the second month switch from 2% to 1%, and then 1% to skim. Within three months you will have succeeded without making a huge adjustment. This same example can be applied to almost any no-fat option products that are available to us, like sour cream, yogurt, mayonnaise, etc.

Most importantly, when preparing a meal, make sure you garnish. This is extremely important for enjoying and experiencing food to the fullest. Eating is not just about taste, texture, and aroma – it is also about appearance. I always preach to my culinary students "the eyes eat first". If something looks great, you are sending signals to your brain advising that it's going to taste great. The same happens in reverse. If someone serves you a bowl of blue coloured mush, it doesn't matter how good it might taste, you have already convinced yourself that it will taste terrible!

Dear Chef Dez:
My New Year's resolution, as it has been for many years, is to lose weight. I find this very hard to do because I love food, and was wondering if you could offer some suggestions?
Susan M.
Langley, BC

Dear Susan:
I myself have battled between the balance of food enticement and weight stability. It seemed I had tried every diet/weight program available and nothing worked for any length of time. I finally just started making my own conscious efforts on a daily basis to make healthier choices towards food and exercise. I made food with intense flavour and low fat to conquer my cravings. Doing this, along with an exercise program, I lost 50 pounds in six months over 4 years ago, and have not gained any back since. My biggest revelation was to not look at the final goal I was trying to achieve. Instead I focus on each day as it comes, and only on that day. Eventually, all those days of healthy choices add up. If you quit trying, your chances of success are guaranteed to be zero – you have a chance as long as you try. Don't give up!

Cajun Chicken with Kiwi Salsa

Full colour photo available at www.chefdez.com

"Discarding the seeds and the inner white membrane from the jalapeno will make the salsa much milder"

KIWI SALSA

4 kiwi fruit, peeled and diced small
¼ (one quarter) cup small diced red bell pepper
¼ (one quarter) cup small diced yellow bell pepper
¼ (one quarter) cup small diced red onion
1 garlic clove crushed
½ (one half) jalapeno pepper, diced small
Juice from ½ (one half) lime
Salt, pepper, and sugar* to season

1 Stir salsa ingredients together and refrigerate until needed. *The sugar will not only make the salsa seem milder, but it will also help to bring all the flavours together.
2 Makes approximately 2 cups of salsa

CAJUN CHICKEN

¼ (one quarter) cup paprika
2 tsp ground black pepper
2 tsp ground dried oregano
2 tsp salt
½ (one half) tsp cayenne pepper
4 to 6 boneless, skinless chicken breasts

1 Preheat oven to 400 degrees.
2 Combine first five ingredients together in a small bowl. Pour onto a dinner plate or a small baking sheet.
3 Dredge chicken in spice mixture until thoroughly coated on both sides.
4 Place chicken breasts on a baking sheet and bake for approximately 20 to 22 minutes until cooked through
5 Plate each chicken breast with a couple spoonfuls of salsa.

Makes 4 to 6 portions

Fat Free Sweet Potato Bisque

Full colour photo available at www.chefdez.com

"This soup is so rich from the sweet potato it will seem like it has cream in it, but there is no added fat whatsoever!"

1kg orange sweet potato, peeled, diced 1cm
1 tbsp dark brown sugar
1 tbsp salt
½ (one half) tsp ground nutmeg
¼ (one quarter) tsp ground cloves
¼ (one quarter) tsp ground white pepper
3 ½ (three and one half) cups skim milk

FOR GARNISH

¼ (one quarter) cup no-fat sour cream
1 tbsp skim milk
Fresh parsley, finely chopped

1 Steam the diced sweet potato over boiling water for 20 minutes until fully cooked and tender.
2 Discard the water, and place the cooked sweet potato into a heavy bottomed pot, off the heat.
3 Add the brown sugar, salt, nutmeg, cloves, and white pepper to the sweet potato and combine thoroughly with a potato masher, ensuring no lumps.
4 Once fully mashed, start adding 1 ½ (one and one half) cups of the skim milk slowly while continuing to mash with the potato masher. Switch to a whisk, turn the heat to medium, and blend in the remaining 2 cups of skim milk, mixing thoroughly.
5 Stir occasionally over medium heat until completely heated through. Taste and adjust the seasonings if necessary.
6 While soup is heating, combine the sour cream with the tablespoon of milk.
7 Portion the soup into bowls and drizzle small amounts of the sour cream mixture on each portion. Drag a toothpick back and forth across the surface to create a beautiful design.
8 Sprinkle with chopped parsley and serve immediately.

Makes approximately 6 portions as a first course

Fresh Guacamole

"Avocado Salsa at its best – chunky and full of flavour! The lime juice will help to keep the avocados from oxidizing (turning brown)."

2 soft avocados
Juice from 1 large lime
1/4 (one quarter) yellow bell pepper, finely diced
1/4 (one quarter) red bell pepper, finely diced
1/4 (one quarter) red onion, finely diced
½ (one half) jalapeno pepper, minced
1 garlic clove, crushed
½ (one half) tsp ground cumin
½ (one half) tsp sambal oelek
½ (one half) tsp sugar
Salt & pepper, to taste

1. Cut, pit, and peel the avocados. Mash them in a medium bowl with the lime juice.
2. Add all of the other ingredients to the bowl and mix together. Refrigerate until needed.

Low Fat Filled Crêpes

"If you don't like the texture of cottage cheese, then puree it in a food processor or blender until smooth"

LOW FAT FILLING

2 cups low fat (or no fat) cottage cheese
2 to 3 tsp vanilla extract
Splenda brand sweetener, to taste
Ground cinnamon, to taste
Pinch of salt
Assortment of chopped fresh fruit or berries

CRÊPE BATTER:

½ cup (one half) all-purpose flour
½ (one half) cup milk
¼ (one quarter) cup lukewarm water
2 eggs
2 tbsp melted butter
1 ½ (one and a half) tbsp white sugar
Pinch of salt

Butter for the pan

1. Mix the cottage cheese together with the vanilla, sweetener, cinnamon, and salt.
2. Store in the refrigerator until needed.
3. Combine all the batter ingredients. Mix until smooth – a blender or food processor works perfectly. Place the batter in a container suitable for pouring. *Cover and allow to rest for half an hour, or refrigerate for up to 24 hours.*
4. Place a non-stick pan over medium heat and coat with a bit of butter.
5. Stir the batter briefly. For each crêpe, pour about 2 - 3 tbsp of the batter into the hot pan – immediately lift the pan and start rolling the batter evenly over the pan surface. Cook until it is set and the bottom is golden before flipping it over to brown the other side.
6. Remove from the pan and continue cooking all your crepes- keep them stacked to keep warm.
7. To serve: place a couple spoonfuls of cottage cheese mixture on the center of each crêpe and roll into tubes. The fresh fruit/berries can either go inside the crêpe or on top of the rolled crêpes. Having the fruit on the outside makes for a much nicer presentation.

Makes approximately 8 crêpes

Poached Salmon with No Fat Yogurt Dill Sauce

Full colour photo available at www.chefdez.com

"Since the poaching liquid is not boiled, this recipe still contains alcohol from the wine."

½ (one half) cup no fat yogurt
½ (one half) cup no fat sour cream
2 tbsp finely chopped fresh dill
1 tsp prepared horseradish
Pinch of salt & white pepper
750ml bottle of white wine
600g to 800g boneless salmon filet, cut into 4 portions
Lemon zest and slices, for garnish

1 In a small bowl, combine the yogurt, sour cream, dill, horseradish, salt and pepper. Let stand at room temperature.

2 Pour the wine into a large nonstick saucepan. Heat over medium-low heat until wisps of steam arise from the surface – do not boil.

3 Slide the salmon portions into the hot wine. Cook for approximately 5 to 12 minutes (depending on the thickness of the filets) until fully cooked through. If the filets are not completely covered by the wine, they will need to be carefully flipped over to cook the salmon completely.

4 Remove the salmon carefully from the wine is it will be very fragile. Serve each portion with a dollop of the yogurt dill sauce, and garnish with lemon zest and slices.

Makes 4 portions

15

Spicing Up
Your Winter Meals

The winter months are the perfect time to add a little "kick" to your menu at home. It is very satisfying to curl up with a bowl of comfort food when the weather is blustering cold, and making it spicier will warm you up even more. Several methods and resources are available to accomplish adding "fire to your fork".

The most overused methods of spicing up a dish is the addition of dried crushed chilies or dried ground cayenne pepper. Do you know which spice jars I am referring to? The ones that have not been replenished for years and years. Okay, maybe I'm exaggerating (slightly), but contrary to popular belief dried spices do not last forever. They eventually loose their punch. Always replenish your stock of dried spices and herbs approximately every six to eight months to ensure freshness and flavour stimulating ability. Bulk spice sections at supermarkets make this very manageable and cost efficient.

Dried crushed chilies are good for adding heat to a recipe, but they have a downside. Their heat producing traits are not fully developed until they have been given time to re-hydrate and release their flavour. Although this a good standby when you have no other available options, there are many other ways.

One product I absolutely love and recommend is Sambal Oelek. This is a crushed chili sauce product, and therefore needs no re-hydration. I use it in countless recipes and it's fantastic for adding instant heat to a dish or a different dimension of flavour. Once the jar is opened it will last in the refrigerator for a long time. Available in the Asian food isle of almost every major grocery store, this product is a must for your kitchen.

Fresh chili peppers have been ever increasing in popularity, and consequently the available options in produce sections have multiplied. They range in varying degrees of hotness with Anaheims being one of the milder options. Jalapenos or Chipotles supply a moderate amount of heat with Scotch Bonnets and Habenaros being the hottest. The amount of heat that a pepper provides is measured scientifically in Scoville units developed by a Professor Wilber L. Scoville in 1912. The majority of this heat comes from not only the seeds, but the inner whitish membranes as well. For flavour with less heat, discard these inner portions. When handling hot peppers, be certain to not touch your eyes or other sensitive areas. Make sure to wash your hands thoroughly upon completion. I find that cold water and soap works the best. If hot water is used, the pores in your skin enlarge trapping the pepper oils in your fingers. One of the best precautions is to wear latex gloves, especially when handling extremely hot peppers.

If the thought of using fresh hot peppers sounds too much like work, there are a number of hot sauces on the market to ease your preparation. I tend to stay away from hot sauces with funny cartoon pictures and "off-the-cuff" names, and stick to old favourites like Tabasco and Frank's Red Hot.

> Dear Chef Dez:
> Is it just me, or do you find that jalapeno peppers aren't as hot as they used to be?
>> John M.
>> Chilliwack, BC

> Dear John:
> You are absolutely right. When I was a teenager, it was considered daring to order these fiery green rings on nachos, and downing three or four slices was a feat in itself. I won't reveal how long ago that was, but the demand for these peppers have grown considerably over the years. Through some investigation, I learned that they are now cultivated to be milder. This is done to expand the appeal of this pepper to a larger consumer market and thus increase sales even further. For those of us who enjoy jalapenos really hot, we now must eat more of them or switch to hotter peppers.

Cajun Chicken with Black Bean Succotash

Full colour photo available at www.chefdez.com

"Succotash is traditionally a side-dish made with steamed lima beans"

CAJUN CHICKEN

¼ (one quarter) cup paprika
2 tsp ground black pepper
2 tsp ground dried oregano
2 tsp salt
½ (one half) tsp cayenne pepper
4 chicken breasts
1 tbsp butter
1 tbsp olive oil
2 large garlic cloves, crushed

> Combine first five ingredients together in a small bowl. Pour onto a dinner plate or a small cookie sheet.
>
> Add butter, oil and garlic to a heavy bottomed pan. Melt at medium/low heat until butter begins to foam.
>
> Dredge chicken in spice mixture until thoroughly coated on both sides.
>
> Place chicken in pan and cook at medium/low heat for approximately 8 to 10 minutes per side until thoroughly done.

BLACK BEAN SUCCOTASH

3 cups frozen corn kernels thawed and drained
1 - 540 ml can black beans rinsed and drained
1 small zucchini quartered and sliced thin
1 large red bell pepper diced small
1 jalapeno pepper diced small
2 garlic cloves crushed
½ (one half) cup cilantro coarsely chopped
3 tsp salt
Pinch of ground black pepper
2 tbsp olive oil

> Combine all ingredients except oil in a bowl and mix thoroughly. (Jalapeno

seeds and membrane can be eliminated for a milder dish.)

Heat heavy bottom pan over medium heat.

Add vegetable mixture to pan and cook for ten minutes, stirring occasionally.

Mound succotash in the middle of four dinner plates and place a chicken breast on the top of each mound.

Garnish each with a spoonful of sour cream and a sprig of fresh cilantro, if desired.

Makes 4 servings

Chili-Rubbed Chicken & Cornbread

Full colour photo available at www.chefdez.com

"The intense flavour of the Chili-Rubbed Chicken goes perfectly with the mild Cornbread and sour cream."

CHILI-RUBBED CHICKEN

3 tbsp chili powder
1 ½ (one and one half) tbsp dark brown sugar
2 tsp garlic powder
2 tsp paprika
2 tsp salt
2 tsp ground cumin
1 tsp freshly cracked pepper
1 tsp dried oregano
½ (one half) tsp cinnamon
diced small
4 chicken breasts
1 tbsp butter
1 tbsp olive oil
2 large garlic cloves, crushed
Sour Cream & green onion slices for garnish

CORNBREAD

1 cup yellow cornmeal
½ (one half) cup all purpose flour
1 tsp baking powder
¼ (one quarter) tsp baking soda
2 tbsp white sugar
1 cup grated cheddar cheese
1 cup frozen corn kernels
½ (one half) jalapeno, diced small
¼ (one quarter) red bell pepper,

½ (one half) tsp salt
2 eggs, beaten
½ (one half) cup sour cream
½ (one half) cup milk
¼ (one quarter) cup vegetable oil

CORNBREAD

1 Preheat the oven to 400 degrees and spray an 8-inch square pan with baking spray.
2 Place the cornmeal, flour, baking powder, baking soda, sugar, cheese, corn, jalapeno, bell pepper, and salt in a large bowl – mix to combine.
3 Place the eggs, sour cream, milk, and oil in a second bowl – mix to combine.
4 Add the wet ingredients to the dry ingredients, and mix until just combined. Pour into the prepared 8-inch pan and bake for approximately 30 minutes until golden brown and an inserted toothpick comes out clean.

CHICKEN

1 In a small bowl, mix the chili powder, brown sugar, garlic powder, paprika, salt, cumin, pepper, oregano, and cinnamon together and pour onto a large plate.
2 Dredge the chicken in the spice mixture until completely coated.
3 Over medium heat, melt the butter into the oil and crushed garlic in a heavy bottomed nonstick pan.
4 Add the chicken to the pan and cook over medium heat for approximately 8 – 10 minutes per side or until done.

Plating

1 Cut the cornbread into 4 equal squares
2 On each plate, put one piece of cornbread, top it with a chicken breast, a dollop of sour cream, and a sprinkle of green onions.

Makes 4 servings

Indian Butter Chicken

Full colour photo available at www.chefdez.com

"My version of a popular Indian dish"

2 cups canned diced tomatoes, not drained
1 – 156ml can tomato paste
2/3 (two thirds) cup plain yogurt (full fat)

½ (one half) cup ground almonds
4 garlic cloves, crushed
4 tbsp dark brown sugar
3 tsp sambal oelek
3 tsp chili powder
2 tsp garam masala
2 tsp finely minced fresh ginger
1 ½ (one and one half) tsp salt
½ (one half) tsp ground cloves
½ (one half) tsp ground cinnamon
1 kg boneless, skinless chicken thighs – 12
6 green cardamom pods
2 whole bay leaves
6 tbsp butter
1 tbsp canola oil
2 medium onions, thinly sliced
Salt & pepper
½ (one half) cup whipping cream
1 tbsp cornstarch
4 tbsp chopped fresh cilantro
cooked basmati rice

1 In a large mixing bowl, combine together the tomatoes, tomato paste, yogurt, almonds, garlic, brown sugar, sambal oelek, chili powder, garam masala, ginger, salt, cloves, and cinnamon.

2 Cut the chicken into bite-sized pieces and stir in to the mixture.

3 Gently pinch the cardamom pods to open them up a bit and add them whole along with the bay leaves to the chicken mixture.

4 Let marinate in the refrigerator for 1 to 4 hours.

5 In a heavy bottomed pot or large deep skillet, melt the butter and oil together over medium-high heat. Add the onions, season with salt & pepper, and sauté until soft, approximately 3 minutes.

6 Add the chicken & marinade mixture and continue to cook over medium-high heat until the chicken is cooked through, approximately 7 to 10 minutes, stirring occasionally.

7 Remove the whole bay leaves and cardamom pods.

8 Mix the whipping cream and the cornstarch together, and pour into the boiling chicken mixture while stirring. Bring the mixture to a boil once again to

ensure the full thickening power of the cornstarch.

9 Stir in 2 tbsp of the cilantro and serve over rice, garnishing with the remaining cilantro.

Makes 4 to 6 servings

Linguine in Roasted Corn Chipotle Cream Sauce

"The roasted corn with the smokiness of the chipotles makes this a great side dish"

2 ½ (two and one half) cups corn kernels
2 tbsp olive oil
Salt & pepper

2 tbsp olive oil
1 small onion, diced small
6 garlic cloves, minced
2 chipotle peppers (canned), minced
2 tsp salt
½ (one half) tsp fresh cracked pepper
½ (one half) small red bell pepper, diced small
1 tsp sugar
1 ½ (one and one half) cups whipping cream
300g dry linguine, cooked al dente*
Salt & pepper to re-season, if necessary
Freshly chopped parsley, for garnish

1 Toss the corn kernels with the 2 tbsp olive oil and season with salt & pepper. Spread them on a baking sheet and roast in a 425 degree oven for approximately 15 to 25 minutes (depending on if fresh or frozen corn is used). Watch carefully to avoid burning and stir occasionally. They will be done when they are starting to caramelize (turn brown). Remove from the oven.

2 Heat a heavy bottomed, nonstick pan over medium heat. Add the other 2 tbsp of olive oil, the onion, garlic, chipotles, salt, and pepper and sauté until the onion and garlic are soft, 3 to 5 minutes.

3 Add the roasted corn, bell pepper, and sugar and continue to sauté for approximately 1 to 2 minutes more.

4 Stir in the cream and heat to a simmer. Remove from the heat and toss in the freshly cooked linguine. Taste and re-season if necessary.

5 Plate and garnish with fresh chopped parsley.

* Dry linguine is usually cooked for 8 minutes in boiling water for al dente. Make sure to salt the water liberally prior to boiling but do not and oil. Oil will coat the natural starch found on the pasta and prevent the sauce from adhering to it.

Makes 4 to 6 side servings

Quick & Thick 3 Bean Chili

Recipe created by Chef Dez/Gordon Desormeaux

"This is a very fast way to a hearty, flavourful chili. Mixing in refried beans gives you the ability to make a thick chili without simmering for hours."

1 pound lean ground beef

3 tbsp & 1 tsp chili powder

1 tbsp dried oregano

1 tbsp ground cumin

1 tbsp olive oil

2 tsp salt

1 tsp ground cayenne pepper

1 tsp black pepper

1 medium onion, chopped

4 garlic cloves, chopped

1 - 398ml can of refried beans

2 cups frozen corn kernels

1 - 796ml can of diced tomatoes – do not drain

1 - 398ml can of red kidney beans, drained & rinsed

1 - 540ml can of black beans, drained & rinsed

3 tbsp dark brown sugar

2 tsp beef stock paste

½ (one half) cup dark beer

½ (one half) cup grated cheddar cheese, for garnish
½ (one half) cup sour cream, for garnish
Chopped parsley, for garnish (optional)

1 Add the beef, chili powder, oregano, cumin, oil, salt, cayenne, pepper, onion, and garlic to a large heavy bottomed pot.
2 Turn the heat to medium high while mixing thoroughly until the beef is completely cooked.
3 Remove from the heat and incorporate the can of refried beans until it is thoroughly combined.
4 Place the pot back on the heat and add all of the remaining ingredients (except the cheese, sour cream, and parsley), and stir occasionally until it is completely heated through.
5 Serve in bowls with a sprinkle of cheddar, a dollop of sour cream, and a light sprinkling of parsley.

Makes 4 to 6 servings

Southwestern Steak Diane

Full colour photo available at www.chefdez.com

"A classic dish with a Southwestern twist! Increasing or decreasing the amount of chipotle peppers being used can control the spiciness of this dish."

4 Striploin steaks
2 tbsp olive oil
Salt & pepper
8 medium white mushrooms, sliced
2 tsp Worcestershire sauce
1 tbsp butter
1 to 2 chipotle peppers (canned), chopped
2 tbsp finely chopped onion
3 garlic cloves, finely chopped
1 tbsp fresh lemon juice

1 tsp yellow mustard

2 tsp sugar

½ (one half) cup whipping cream

2 oz. Jack Daniels whiskey

Salt & fresh cracked pepper to taste

2 green onions, sliced for garnish

1 Oil the steaks with one tablespoon of the olive oil. Season them with salt & pepper.

2 Heat a heavy bottomed pan over medium to medium-high heat. Add the other tablespoon of olive oil and sear the steaks for approximately 3 to 4 minutes per side for medium-rare to medium steaks.

3 Remove the steaks from the pan and keep them covered to stay warm.

4 Turn the heat to medium and add the mushrooms and Worcestershire sauce and cook for approximately 1 minute.

5 Add the butter, chipotles, onion, and garlic – sauté until the mushrooms are completely cooked, approximately 2 to 3 minutes.

6 Add the lemon juice, mustard, sugar, and whipping cream to the pan. Stir to blend in, add the steaks back to the pan to reheat, and bring to a boil.

7 Once boiling, add the whiskey and ignite with a flame (be careful). Shake the pan until the flames reside and plate the steaks.

8 Return the pan to the burner and over medium-high heat, reduce the sauce until the desired syrupy consistency is reached. Season to taste with salt & pepper, and spoon the sauce over the steaks.

9 Garnish with green onion slices.

Makes 4 servings

16

Setting the Table
for Romance

One of my pet peeves is trying to make dinner reservations on an evening when ninety percent of the general population is also trying to attain the same goal. You may be able to perform this feat without pulling out your hair. However, if bustling crowds and hurried serving staff is not your idea of romance, one can easily create this setting in the comfort of your home.

Staying in for a romantic dinner can be accomplished with little effort and some creative planning. To achieve this successfully, we will focus on three areas: the menu, the table setting, and the room environment.

The menu you decide on does not have to be complicated, however it should be meaningful. Your effort should reflect the compassion you have for this person. The first thought that comes to mind is to prepare their favorite food. If this is a dish that you cannot prepare at home then have it ordered in or pre-purchase parts of it ahead of time to ease your preparation. It's acceptable to not have everything prepared from scratch if it is beyond your means and capability. Your thoughtfulness is the most meaningful ingredient.

Add extra simple courses, rather than just having a main course and dessert. Once again this does not have to be perplexing. A fresh pile of mixed colourful greens with a good dressing makes a great salad course. A few pieces of unique cheeses with some grapes and a small glass of wine make another delicious course. All of the elements to make these extra courses can be purchased direct from the store and assembled together to ease your preparation. Now you can express to your Sweetheart that you made them a "four course romantic dinner". An example of a quick enchanting dessert would be chocolate covered strawberries.

The table setting is very important and should harmonize with the mood you are trying to establish. Candles are a must, but there are other things you can do to make it memorable. Silk rose petals or heart-shaped confetti scattered on the table is a nice touch. Compliment that with red cloth napkins and a love letter tied up with a ribbon, and you will have them swooning. Make sure you have enough pieces of cutlery set to accommodate each course and use your best wine glasses. A glass of wine always looks very elegant; if wine is not desirable, then fill the glass with red juice. A finishing touch on the table would be a fresh bouquet of flowers. Long stemmed red roses are perfect for Valentine's Day, however they will be impressed already by your efforts and carnations or a mixed arrangement will do fine.

The room environment is equally influential. If you have children, make arrangements for them to spend the evening, or at least part of it, with Grandparents or doing other appropriate activities. Be certain that you serve dinner in a light controlled room and have access to music. Favorite cd's are the best option as they eliminate the hassle of having to listen to advertisements on the radio. Lastly, make sure that the room is tidy. It is much harder to set a mood if the area is cluttered with everyday items.

Now that the lights are dimmed and soft music fills the air, look into their candle-lit eyes and smile. Not only because you created a romantic interlude successfully, but also due to no gratuity being required.

Dear Chef Dez:
I want to make chocolate covered strawberries for dessert for a Valentine's dinner, but the last time I tried making them it was a disaster. Even though I took them out of the refrigerator ahead of time, the chocolate was still too hard and it broke off the berries with the first bite and fell onto the plate. What am I doing wrong?
Chris D.
Abbotsford, BC

Dear Chris:
When melting your chocolate for dipping, melt butter in with the chocolate as well. Room temperature butter is much softer than room temperature chocolate, and thus will create a more palatable bite and will adhere to the berries. I normally add 50% of the weight of chocolate being used with butter. For example, if you are melting four ounces of chocolate, then also melt in two ounces of butter.

Amaretto Truffles with Vanilla Pastry Cream

Full colour photo available at www.chefdez.com

"This chocolate dessert is well worth the effort of getting your hands a bit dirty"

TRUFFLES

1 cup semi-sweet chocolate chips
¼ (one quarter) cup butter
2 tbsp icing sugar, sifted
2 tbsp cream cheese, room temperature
3 tbsp amaretto
Unsweetened cocoa powder
Sliced almonds, crushed

1. In a double boiler, gently melt the chocolate and the butter together until smooth and fully combined.
2. Remove from the heat and stir in the icing sugar, then the cream cheese until fully combined and lump free.
3. Stir in the amaretto and chill in the refrigerator until solid (min. 2 hours).
4. Using a spoon, quickly scoop out a heaping teaspoon of the mixture, roll and press it into a ball in your hands, and then roll it in cocoa powder or almonds. Do each one individually and set aside before moving on to the next one, to help prevent melting of the chocolate.

VANILLA PASTRY CREAM

1 cup milk
¼ (one quarter) cup sugar
1 tsp vanilla extract
1/8 (one eighth) tsp salt
3 egg yolks
1 tbsp flour, sifted
1 ½ (one and one half) tsp cornstarch, sifted
More amaretto and fresh mint leaves for garnish

1. In a heavy bottomed pot, mix the milk, sugar, vanilla, and salt together and bring to a boil over medium-high heat, stirring frequently.
2. Beat the egg yolks with the flour and cornstarch until it becomes pale yellow.

3 Starting very slowly, gradually add the hot milk to the beaten yolks to ensure that the eggs don't get too hot all at once.

4 Return the mixture to the pot and bring to a boil over medium heat while whisking constantly, approximately 2 to 3 minutes. It is at the boiling point that the mixture will thicken. Spoon into a separate bowl and chill.

For each portion, place a dollop of pastry cream in a martini glass, and nestle 3 truffles in the pastry cream. Drizzle with a teaspoon of amaretto and garnish with a fresh mint leaf.

Makes Approximately 12 – 15 truffles (4 – 5 servings)

Blueberry Cheesecake Crêpes

Full colour photo available at www.chefdez.com

"For breakfast or dessert – these crêpes are to die for!"

CHEESECAKE FILLING & SAUCE:

1-cup cream cheese
½ (one half) cup ricotta cheese
Zest of 1 lemon finely chopped
Juice of ½ (one half) lemon
1 tsp vanilla
1 cup icing sugar sifted
3 cups blueberries

Stir the cream cheese until smooth and pliable. Stir in the ricotta. Add the lemon zest, lemon juice, vanilla and icing sugar. Blend until smooth.

Filling: use 1 cup of this cream cheese mixture combined with 2 cups of the blueberries.

Sauce: use the remaining cream cheese mixture combined with the 1 remaining cup of blueberries.

Refrigerate both bowls until thoroughly chilled.

BLUEBERRY TOPPING:

2 cups fresh or frozen blueberries

1/3 (one third) cup granulated sugar
Juice of 1 lemon
2 tbsp cold water
1 ½ (one and a half) tbsp cornstarch
Pinch nutmeg

> Combine blueberries, sugar and lemon juice in a pot over medium/high heat. Mash berries a little while cooking, for approximately 3 - 4 minutes.
> Combine water and cornstarch together in a small bowl, and whisk into the boiling berry mixture. Stir until thick and remove from the heat.
> Stir in nutmeg.

CRÊPE BATTER:

½ cup (one half) all-purpose flour
½ (one half) cup milk
¼ (one quarter) cup lukewarm water
2 eggs
2 tbsp melted butter
1 ½ (one and a half) tbsp white sugar
Pinch of salt

Butter for the pan

> Combine all the batter ingredients. Mix until smooth – a blender or food processor works perfectly. Place the batter in a container suitable for pouring. *Cover and allow to rest for one half hour, or refrigerate for up to 24 hours.*
> Place a non-stick pan over medium heat and coat with a bit of butter.
> Stir the batter briefly. For each crêpe, pour about 2 - 3 tbsp of the batter into the hot pan – immediately lift the pan and start rolling the batter evenly over the pan surface. Cook until it is set and the bottom is golden before flipping it over to brown the other side.
> Remove from the pan and continue cooking all your crepes- keep them stacked to keep warm.

To Assemble

Spoon some of the filling onto one side of a crêpe. Roll 1 to 3 of these crêpes per portion. Spoon some of the cheesecake sauce over the crêpes, and then top with the blueberry sauce.

Garnish with more fresh blueberries, powdered sugar, and a mint leaf if desired.

Makes approximately 8 crêpes

Cajun Pan-Fried Oysters

"Two aphrodisiacs in one dish – oysters & spice!"

1 227g container of fresh oysters (approximately 6-7)
½ (one half) cup flour
1 egg
1/8 (one eighth) cup milk
¼ (one quarter) cup olive oil
Small chopped red pepper and chopped parsley for garnish

BREADING

12 stoned wheat crackers
2 tbsp paprika
2 tsp cayenne pepper
1 tsp salt
¼ (one quarter) tsp black pepper

1 Prepare breading by processing the five ingredients in a food processor on high speed for approximately 30 seconds.
2 Gently rinse the oysters under running water and drain.
3 Put the flour on a plate.
4 Beat the egg and milk together in a small bowl.
5 Bread the oysters as follows:
   a Roll each oyster in the flour until well coated.
   b Dip in the egg wash.
   c Roll each oyster in the breading and set aside on a clean plate.
6 Heat the olive oil in a heavy-bottomed pan over medium heat.
7 Pan-fry the oysters about 3 to 4 at a time for approximately 1 minute on each side.
8 Set the oysters on clean paper towel for a few seconds to drain.
9 Serve warm with a favorite mayonnaise sauce for dipping. Garnish the plates with the diced red pepper, chopped parsley, and a sprinkle of paprika.

Makes 2 servings as an appetizer

Grilled Brie & Apple Pizza

Full colour photo available at www.chefdez.com (PICTURED ON FRONT COVER)

"Grilling the pizza on the barbeque gives it a flame licked taste that is reminiscent of cooking it in a wood fired forno oven"

PIZZA CRUST

2½ (two and one half) cups all-purpose flour

2 tsp instant yeast

2 tsp sugar

¾ (three quarters) tsp salt

¾ (three quarters) cup + 2 tbsp water, room temperature

2 tbsp extra-virgin olive oil

PIZZA SAUCE

1 cup whole pitted dates

3 garlic cloves, peeled

250g pkg. cream cheese, room temperature

2 tbsp extra-virgin olive oil

½ (one half) tsp salt

TOPPINGS

3 Gala apples, quartered, cored & sliced thin

1 tbsp lemon juice

¼ (one quarter) cup cold water

400g Brie cheese

36 large cooked prawns

4 green onions, thinly sliced diagonally (greens only)

salt & fresh cracked pepper

Pizza Crust

1 Mix the flour, yeast, sugar, and salt in a large bowl. Add the water & olive oil and mix until it starts coming together. Turn out onto a lightly floured surface and knead for 7-8 minutes until smooth and elastic.

2 Place the dough in a lightly oiled bowl, cover with plastic wrap, and let sit for approximately one hour until doubled in volume. Make sure this is done in a warm

place with no drafts. While the dough is proofing, prepare sauce and toppings.

3 Alternately, you can use a bread-maker by putting in all of the crust ingredients and selecting the 'dough' setting.

4 Punch down the dough. Remove from the bowl and divide into four equal portions. Roll out each portion into a roughly shaped 8 to 10 inch circle.

Pizza Sauce

1 Place the dates and garlic cloves in a food processor and process on high speed until finely minced, approximately 1 minute.

2 Scrape down the sides of the processor and add the cream cheese, olive oil and salt. Process on high speed until fully combined, approximately 30 seconds.

Cooking & Assembly

1 Add the apples slices to the mixture of lemon juice and water to keep from going brown.

2 Cut off the side, round edge of the rind from the Brie (leaving the top and bottom rind in tact), and slice the Brie into thin slices.

3 Place a perforated grill insert on top of your barbeque grill and spray with baking spray. Preheat over medium-high heat for approximately two minutes.

4 Place one pizza dough round on the grill insert and lower the heat to medium. Cook the one side for approximately 5 minutes until golden brown and lightly charred (while gently piercing any air bubbles with a fork).

5 Flip the crust over and turn off the heat. Carefully spread ¼ (one quarter) of the pizza sauce over the surface of the crust. Layer ¼ (one quarter) of the apple slices (drained) and follow with ¼ (one quarter) of the slices of Brie.

6 Turn on the heat to low, close the cover, and cook for approximately 3 minutes until the Brie starts to melt.

7 Add 9 prawns, slices of green onion, salt and fresh cracked pepper to the pizza. Re-close the cover to the barbeque and continue to cook for approximately 2 more minutes to heat up the prawns.

8 Remove from the grill and serve immediately.

9 Repeat 3 times for the other pizzas.

Makes 4, 8-10" pizzas

Marscapone Stuffed Poached Pears

Full colour photo available at www.chefdez.com

"This a dessert to eat with a knife, fork and spoon so you get every drop"

FILLING

¾ (three quarter) cup marscapone cheese
¼ (one quarter) cup icing sugar
1 tbsp white sugar
1 tbsp orange brandy
2 tsp fresh lemon juice

1 ½ (one and one half) cups full-bodied red wine
1 cup white sugar
1 cinnamon stick, broken in half
10 whole allspice
5 whole cloves
Zest from a large orange
4 Anjou pears

1. Mix the ingredients for the filling, and refrigerate.
2. Add all the other ingredients (except for the pears) to a pot large enough to hold the four pears. Bring to a boil to dissolve the sugar. Reduce heat to low, cover and simmer for 5 minutes to infuse the flavours.
3. Peel the top parts of the pears, and cut the tops off to make a "hat" for the pears (keep the stems on for presentation). Hollow out the cores of the pears with a melon baller, just deep enough to remove the seeds – keeping the bottom of the pears in tact. Now peel the pears. *It is important to keep the pear's flesh from being exposed too long to prevent oxidization (turning brown).
4. Add the pears and the pear tops to the wine mixture, and poach over medium-low heat, covered, and occasionally turning the pears and ladling hot wine over the pears. Poach for 20 minutes total.
5. Remove the pot from the heat, keep covered, and let the pears cool in the wine, still occasionally turning the pears and ladling wine over them as they cool to help keep them evenly coloured.
6. Once they have hit room temperature (or slightly warm), slice a small amount off the bottom of the pears to help them stand on their own, and

place them upright in small serving bowls.

7 Fill the pears with the marscapone mixture, and place the pears tops back onto the pears.

8 Strain the wine mixture through a fine mesh strainer, and return the liquid to the pot. Discard the solids. Heat the liquid over medium-high heat until it has reduced by about half in volume and has become syrupy, approximately 5 – 10 minutes.

9 Ladle the desired amount of hot syrup over the pears, and enjoy!

Makes 4 servings.

Rack of Lamb with Rosemary Roasted Potatoes

Full colour photo available at www.chefdez.com

"A beautiful presentation that will leave them breathless. Rack of lamb is not difficult to prepare."

1 pound baby new potatoes
2 to 3tbsp olive oil
Two stalks of fresh rosemary or 1 tbsp dry rosemary
6 whole cloves of garlic peeled
Salt and fresh cracked pepper to taste
2 stalks of fresh rosemary for garnish

1 Pre-heat oven to 450 degrees.

2 Wash and dry potatoes, cutting larger ones in half to allow for even cooking. Place them in a bowl with garlic cloves.

3 Drizzle with olive oil.

4 Strip rosemary from stalks and sprinkle over potatoes.

5 Season generously with salt and fresh cracked pepper.

6 Toss to coat.

7 Place on a cookie sheet and bake for 30-40 minutes until fully cooked, stirring half way through.

2 racks of lamb approximately ¾ of a pound each, frenched

2 tbsp olive oil

Salt and freshly cracked pepper to taste

½ (one half) tsp beef stock paste

½ (one half) cup full bodied, dry, red wine

½ (one half) tsp sugar

2 to 3 tbsp whipping cream

1. Pre-heat heavy bottomed pan over medium/high heat.
2. Place racks of lamb in a bowl, drizzle with oil. Season with salt and pepper on both sides.
3. When pan is hot place lamb racks in pan to sear.
4. Sear on both sides and ends. Approximately five minutes total.
5. Place in a pan on a wire rack and roast in oven for fifteen minutes (medium rare).
6. Turn heat for pan to medium.
7. Add beef stock paste to pan and deglaze with red wine.
8. Add the sugar and stir in the cream.
9. Reduce approximately 1 to 2 minutes, until syrupy.
10. Transfer immediately to serving dish from hot pan to prevent further reduction.
11. Remove lamb from oven and let rest for five minutes to allow the meat to retain its juices.

Plating:

Mound potatoes and garlic cloves in center of each plate.

Cut lamb racks between bones, into chops, and arrange in a standing circular display around potatoes.

Drizzle chops and plate rim with wine reduction and garnish each plate with a stalk of fresh rosemary.

Makes 2 servings

Seafood Angel-Hair Pasta

"My version of a dish I always ordered years ago at a favorite Italian restaurant"

1 small to medium carrot, diced very small

1 large celery stalk, diced very small

½ (one half) medium white onion, diced very small
6 cloves of garlic, crushed
2 tbsp olive oil
28 fl oz. can of diced tomatoes
1 cup full-bodied red wine
1 tbsp & 1 tsp white sugar
¼ (one quarter) cup whipping cream
Salt & fresh cracked pepper to taste
12 – 16 live mussels, cleaned
20 – 30 small scallops
10 – 12 large raw prawns, cleaned
Angel-hair pasta
Parsley, for garnish

1. Heat a heavy bottomed pot over medium heat.
2. Add the 2 tablespoons of olive oil.
3. Add carrot, celery, onion, and garlic. Gently season with salt & pepper, and sweat until soft but not brown, about 2 to 3 minutes; stirring frequently.
4. Add the can of tomatoes (not drained).
5. Turn heat to high and reduce until liquid is almost gone; watching closely and stirring frequently while gradually lowering heat from high to medium-high; about 10 minutes.
6. Add the red wine and reduce again over medium-high heat; stirring occasionally while gradually lowering heat to medium; about 5 to 10 minutes.
7. Stir in the sugar.
8. Stir in the cream and turn down the heat to low. Season with salt and pepper to taste.
9. Add the scallops and the mussels; cover; turn up the heat to medium and cook until the mussels have opened.
10. Once the mussels have opened, remove the cover and add the prawns. Cook further only until prawns are just barely cooked (they will turn pink) – do not over cook or prawns will become rubbery.
11. Remove from the heat and toss in the cooked angel-hair pasta.
12. Plate the pasta with tongs. Arrange an equal amount of mussels around each mound of pasta and add more of the sauce. (Discard any mussels that didn't open)
13. Garnish with fresh chopped parsley and serve immediately.

Makes 3 to 4 servings

17

Bacon Adds Sizzling Flavour

For those of you who have not yet heard, bacon is not just a breakfast side dish. Although greatly feared by vegetarians and dieters alike, bacon is a wonderfully versatile addition to numerous recipes for increased flavour complexity. The versatility I'm referring to extends further than the use of the rendered fat to fry your eggs in. The inclusion of bacon in recipes has matured greatly from those archaic past uses.

Salads are a great example of this. Heaven forbid that the first thing entering your mind is "simulated bacon flavoured bits" reminiscent of antiquated salad bars. True flavour comes from real genuine bacon strips fried until crispy and crumbled. Many salads today that are garnished with bacon are often complimented with other contrasting flavours such as apple slices, for example. Even warm dressings can be made with the leftover bacon fat in place of the oil. Just add an acidic ingredient such as wine vinegar, and other supporting flavours, to capture the essence of a classic dressing.

Many soups are also improved with the inclusion of bacon. The depth of flavour gained by this simple addition is incredible, as long as moderation is practiced. A complimenting flavour should always be in the background, and never the main attraction, of a dish. The rendered fat can also be utilized in the making of a thickening roux if suitable. A *roux* (pronounced "roo") is a mixture of equal parts of fat and flour by weight used to thicken soups or sauces.

However, the incorporation of bacon is definitely not limited to just salads and soups, as it can be included in almost any savoury recipe.

Most of the bacon that we purchase pre-sliced in 500g packages is obtained from the belly of the pig. This can be identified by the considerable amount of fat content. Back bacon however is fairly lean and meaty, and is aptly named from its origin. All bacon is quite salty as it is always salt cured or brined and usually smoked. Thus the practice of seasoning a dish that incorporates bacon should be mostly reserved until the end of the cooking process.

For years, bacon has also been used in protecting other meats from drying out during the cooking process. Lean red meat roasts and sometimes even whole fish are wrapped in a bacon barrier prior to cooking. The fatty consistency is perfect for supplying enough juices to keep these main entrées moist and flavourful. This procedure is also perfect for roasting turkey. Rather than lining the outside of the turkey with bacon, separate the skin from the breast meat and insert bacon slices between the two. Roast as normal with the breast side up, and the bacon will help insulate the delicate light meat from losing its juices.

There are obvious health concerns to an over abundant consumption of bacon in our daily diets, and controlled temperance should be practiced. This being said, Elvis Presley's favorite accompanying sauce with his biscuits was "red-eye gravy". This is made by adding a cup of black coffee to the rendered fat from a pound of bacon.

> *Dear Chef Dez:*
> *I have come across a chicken recipe that lists "lardons" as one of the ingredients, can you tell me what this is?*
>
> *Craig C.*
> *Abbotsford, BC*

> *Dear Craig:*
> *Lardons is a French culinary term for bacon that has been diced, blanched, and fried. The blanching process is performed to partially precook the bacon and to eliminate some of the fat content before adding it to a recipe.*

Bacon & Cheddar Corn Chowder

Full colour photo available at www.chefdez.com

"This full flavoured soup is fast, simple, and hearty! Great with big chunks of crusty bread for dipping!"

PART "A"

6 slices bacon, sliced ¼ inch

PART "B"

1 medium onion, diced small
4 cloves garlic, minced
1 large carrot, sliced thin
2 large celery stalks, sliced thin
4 cups corn kernels
1 tbsp olive oil
1 tbsp butter
2 tsp dried tarragon
1 tsp fried oregano
4 tsp salt
1 tbsp sugar
1.5 tsp pepper, freshly cracked
½ (one half) tsp sambal oelek

PART "C"

2 large russet potatoes,
diced ½ inch

PART "D"

¼ (one quarter) cup flour
2 cups milk
2 cups heavy cream
½ (one half) red bell pepper,
diced small
2 cups grated old cheddar
¼ (one quarter) cup chopped
fresh parsley
plus more chopped parsley
for garnish

1 Cook bacon in a large heavy bottomed pot over medium-high heat until crisp. Remove the bacon with a slotted spoon and reserve for garnish.

2 Add all the ingredients in Part B to the rendered bacon fat in the pot. Stir to combine and once the butter is melted, cover and turn the heat down to medium to sweat the vegetables until soft, approximately 5 minutes – do not brown the vegetables.

3 Steam the diced potatoes for approximately 8 to 10 minutes – do not over cook.

4 After sweating the vegetables, remove the lid and stir in the flour. Cook for approximately 2 to 3 minutes to remove the starchy taste of the flour.

5 To avoid lumps, stir the milk in gradually to the flour/vegetable mixture, and add the heavy cream. Partially puree with a hand blender.

6 Add the steamed potatoes, diced bell pepper, and 1 cup of the grated cheddar.

Bring to a simmer over medium heat, stirring frequently to avoid burning. Stir in ¼ (one quarter) cup of parsley.

7 Garnish each bowl with the remaining grated cheddar, chopped parsley, and the reserved bacon pieces.

Makes 6 to 8 servings

Bacon Wrapped Asparagus

Full colour photo available at www.chefdez.com

1 pound fresh thin asparagus spears
2 tbsp olive oil
2 tbsp balsamic vinegar
Salt & Pepper
8 to 10 bacon slices
Baking Spray

1 Trim the "woody" ends off the asparagus spears (approximately one quarter or one third off) and discard.

2 Place the asparagus tips in a dish large enough to accommodate the length of them. Pour the oil and vinegar over the asparagus, season with salt and pepper, and toss together.

3 Let the asparagus stand in the marinade for ½ (one half) to 2 hours at room temperature.

4 Preheat the oven to 400 degrees.

5 Slice each bacon slice in half, lengthwise.

6 With each half bacon slice, wrap 2 or 3 of the asparagus spears together. Stretch the bacon slightly as you wrap the asparagus snuggly with the half bacon slices.

7 Spray a baking sheet with baking spray, and lay the wrapped asparagus on the baking sheet.

8 Bake for approximately 15 to 25 minutes (depending on the thickness of your asparagus) until the asparagus is tender and the bacon is cooked.

Makes 4 servings

Grandma G's Potato Soup

"Another classic recipe from my Grandma. This is one of my Mom's childhood favorites"

¼ (one quarter) pound bacon, cut into ¼ (one quarter) inch pieces
1 small onion, diced
3 to 4 stalks of celery, sliced (including the leaves)
2 tbsp finely chopped parsley
3 tbsp flour
1 cup chicken stock
5 cups water
4 medium potatoes, diced ½ (one half) inch
1 cup cream
1 cup milk
Salt & pepper to taste
More finely chopped parsley for garnish

1. Sauté the bacon pieces in a heavy bottomed pot over medium heat until crisp.
2. Add the onion, celery, and parsley and season with salt & pepper, and sauté for another 10 minutes.
3. Add the flour and stir until a smooth paste forms; cooking for about two minutes.
4. Gradually add the chicken stock & water while stirring to prevent lumps.
5. Add the potatoes and bring to a slow boil. Turn the heat to low and simmer for approximately ½ hour until potatoes are tender.
6. Take a potato masher and mash the potatoes into the soup – do not mash too much as you still want some texture.
7. Add the cream and milk and cook over low heat until hot, stirring occasionally.
8. Season to taste with salt and pepper. Garnish with parsley.

Red Eye Gravy

"A classic favorite of Elvis Presley. Not something you want to eat often, but worth trying."

Fat rendered from cooking 1 pound of bacon

1 cup black coffee

1. After removing the bacon from cooking it, let the remaining fat cool in the pan slightly.
2. Stir in the cup of black coffee and increase heat to medium.
3. Continue to cook, stirring occasionally, until it has reduced by half in volume.
4. Traditionally eaten with biscuits in the morning.

Makes approximately 1 ½ (one and one half) cups

Warm Bacon Dressing

"The greens you dress this on will get a bit wilted, so only dress them immediately before serving"

Rendered fat from ½ (one half) pound bacon, approximately ½ (one half) cup
3 tbsp apple cider vinegar
1 to 2 tbsp maple syrup
2 tsp Dijon or grainy mustard
½ (one half) tsp dried thyme leaves
Fresh cracked pepper, to season

1. Add all the ingredients to the rendered bacon fat (make sure that the bacon fat is not too hot or the hot fat will splatter you when you add these ingredients).
2. Heat over medium heat until very warm while stirring together.
3. Serve immediately over your choice of greens (mixed greens or spinach leaves are fantastic).

Glossary of Terms

Al denté – Italian for *"to the tooth"*. The term most commonly used to describe the cooking of pasta, meaning it should not be overcooked and have a bit of resistance when bitten into.

Baguette – a long thin French loaf of bread.

Beef Stock Paste – beef stock/broth that has been concentrated down to a paste consistency. Allows one to add intense flavour without adding liquid to a recipe.

Blind Bake – means to pre-bake a pie shell with no filling in it.

Bocconcini Cheese – small balls of fresh mozzarella cheese usually stored in small tubs of brine.

Bruscetta – toasted slices of baguette topped with a variety of ingredients and served as an appetizer.

Button Mushrooms – common white mushrooms.

Cheesecloth – originally used to separate curds from the whey in cheese making, this food-safe perforated cloth has numerous filtering uses in the kitchen.

Chicken Stock Paste – chicken stock/broth that has been concentrated down to a paste consistency. Allows one to add intense flavour without adding liquid to a recipe.

Chipotle Peppers – are smoked jalapeno peppers and are usually packaged in cans.

Deglaze – to remove the browned bits (fond) in a hot pan by adding a liquid. This lifts the fond off of the pan and it becomes part of the sauce/finished dish.

Demiglaze – technically speaking this should be a combination of half brown sauce with half brown stock and then reduced in volume by half. Now-a-days this term is loosely used in a number of different recipes meaning a reduced sauce.

Double Boiler – a pot or saucepan that has an insert that sits above the water level. This allows to cook with steam as a heat source.

Dredge – to drag through dry ingredients to coat.

Emulsifier – an ingredient, such as egg yolks, that helps bind oil and liquids together.

Enoki Mushroom – one of the smallest and most delicate varieties. They grow in clusters of small white caps on long thin stems that are usually 6 to 10 centimetres long.

Frenched Rack of Lamb – bones on the rack have been cleaned of tissue/fat for better presentation.

Melon Baller – a kitchen utensil that has a half sphere stainless steel end that is commonly used to create round balls of solid fruits like melons.

Oyster Mushroom - delicate fluted mushrooms with their stems usually grouped together. They have a mild flavour that some say is reminiscent of oysters.

Portabella Mushroom - very large with their tops ranging anywhere from 7 to 12 centimetres and are known as the steak of all mushrooms.

Reduce/Reduction – to decrease in volume by the process of evaporation. As steam rises from a pan/pot, water is being released and the residual product has intensified flavour and is smaller in quantity.

Sambal Oelek – a crushed chili product that comes in a liquid/paste form. It can usually be found in any major grocery store down the Asian food isle or Imported foods isle.

Shallot – a variety of onion that is smaller and milder than regular onions.

Shitake Mushroom - dark brown mushrooms originated in Asia. They have a smoky and somewhat nutty flavor, and the tough woody stems are usually discarded.

tbsp – abbreviation for tablespoon.

tsp - abbreviation for teaspoon.

Tzatziki – a Greek dipping sauce made from yogurt, cucumber, fresh dill and garlic. Traditionally served on Greek souvlaki.

Vegetable Stock Paste – vegetable stock/broth that has been concentrated down to a paste consistency. Allows one to add intense flavour without adding liquid to a recipe.

White Pepper – is ground peppercorns that have been allowed to mature before harvesting. They are then either soaked or washed in water to remove the outer shell, which produces a white peppercorn with a milder taste. They are frequently utilized to season white sauces to ensure that the appearance of the sauce is not marred with black specs.

Zest – **the coloured outer peel of citrus fruit, not the white bitter pith on the underside of the peel. A tool called a zester or a fine-toothed food grater will help remove this efficiently.**

I

B

Dressings

L

Lamb

M

P

Pasta

R

A

Conversion Chart

VOLUME MEASUREMENTS

3 teaspoons	=	1 tablespoon
2 tablespoons	=	1 fluid ounce
2 fluid ounces	=	¼ (one quarter) cup
¼ (one quarter) cup	=	4 tablespoons
8 fluid ounces	=	1 cup or 16 tablespoons
1 litre	=	4 cups or 32 fluid ounces

WEIGHT MEASUREMENTS

227 grams	=	½ (one half) pound
454 grams	=	1 pound
1 pound	=	16 ounces (not fluid ounces)
1 kilogram	=	2.2 pounds

ISBN 142512019-9